Sonia Gandhi

Tryst with India

Sonia Gandhi

Tryst with India

N.I. Sarkar

ATLANTIC
PUBLISHERS & DISTRIBUTORS (P) LTD

Published by

ATLANTIC

PUBLISHERS & DISTRIBUTORS (P) LTD

B-2, Vishal Enclave, Opp. Rajouri Garden,
New Delhi-110027
Phones : 25413460, 25429987, 25466842

Sales Office
7/22, Ansari Road, Darya Ganj,
New Delhi-110002
Phones : 23273880, 23275880, 23280451
Fax : 91-11-23285873
web : www.atlanticbooks.com
e-mail : info@atlanticbooks.com

ISBN 81-269-0744-4

Printed in India
at Nice Printing Press, Delhi

Acknowledgements

My research for this book took me to various sources and libraries. I am grateful to all who extended help with understanding and affection. I'll be failing in my duty if I do not make a particular mention of All India Congress Committee (AICC) Treasurer Motilal Vora who has been generous in helping me. Rajiv Gandhi Foundation (RGF) also allowed me access to its library. I can't do justice without mentioning the name of United News of India (UNI), which permitted me to use photographs from its archive. I also acknowledge the contribution of National Herald library. It provided me some file photographs. My special thanks go to *National Herald* editor T.V. Venkitachalam for his encouragement and suggestions from time to time.

N.I. SARKAR

Preface

Congress President Sonia Gandhi has been no less than an angel for her party. She has done a miracle by making the party win large number of seats in the 2004 parliamentary elections and forming Congress-led United Progressive Alliance (UPA) Government at the Centre, albeit taking major decisions on her own. After commanding the weak party for just six years she made possible its return to power by dint of her dynamic leadership. In a short period of her political life she has shown her mettle as a great leader. Her wisdom as well as acumen in drawing political strategy is unmatched. Under her stewardship, the Congress party continues to be the nation's sole all-India party. She is in the thick of politics and plays important role in shaping the destiny of the crores of the countrymen.

Sonia has become a strong icon of Indian politics and many of her antagonists have turned into her admirers. It is no mean achievement for a person who, at the beginning, was considered as politically inexperienced and even became a talking point among the opponents for her foreign birth and for knowing little about the country and its people. It is pertinent to say that Sonia hasn't given anyone any scope to think that she is a foreigner. Now she is an Indian citizen and has adopted everything that is characteristic of an Indian—be it dress, food habit and social practice.

Before the parliamentary elections, the Bharatiya Janata Party (BJP) was about as large as the Congress party in terms of vote share, but the BJP couldn't keep its share intact. It used Sonia's foreign origin as ammunition to give her a sure defeat. After coming to power the BJP-led National Democratic Alliance (NDA) Government even set up a committee to amend the Constitution to keep off foreign-born persons from holding high public office. However, the committee couldn't come to a consensus on the issue. So, the BJP failed in its mission to contain her from becoming eligible for such post.

After Rajiv Gandhi, the Congress appeared to have lost its moorings as it was following soft *Hindutva*. Sonia has corrected the aberration in a few years and the Congress regained its image as a party that cuts barriers across religion, caste or region. She made the party stand for the values it is known for. By enacting pro-poor policies, she has already attained the stature of her mother-in-law Indira Gandhi in her short span in politics. In the coming years she is certainly going to ascend greater heights.

Sonia is best example of sacrifice and selfless service for the country. When she turned down the prime minister's post, people recalled a quality of sacrifice that once upon a time was the hallmark of the Congressmen. It is not a small sacrifice in a country where people vie for positions. Even her bitter critics were not prepared for such a decision from her. For this, she will surely continue to reap benefits for a long, long time.

We are enjoying freedom today because of the foresightedness shown by a Britisher, A.O. Hume, who founded the Indian National Congress for building nationalistic passion and the spirit of fighting against injustice perpetrated on the Indians. So, it is absurd to generalize that every foreigner has evil designs in mind. Sonia's refusal to become prime minister is the ultimate proof of her devotion and commitment to the party. As Congress chief, I hope, she will continue to be involved in active politics with enhanced stature and boost the credibility of the party and the UPA Government.

There are few books on her political life. This deficit prompted me to write one on her political journey. I am largely impressed by her affability, courage and selfless service to the party and the country. I offer tribute to her for carving out a place in politics and to be in the service of millions of countrymen. I wish her all the best in her endeavour to reach the pinnacle of cherished goals. I shall be glad if the book *Sonia Gandhi—Tryst with India* is useful to anyone who wants to know more about her.

N.I. SARKAR

Contents

Introduction

Sonia Gandhi—a name that is omnipresent in the country, a name that is inspiration for crores of people and a name that is a guarantee for peace and progress—has become a legend in Indian politics by her extraordinary qualities like renunciation and sacrifice. She may be living in the high security residence at 10, Janpath in the country's capital but her heart goes out to the *aam admi* who toil hard for the development of the country. She has travelled to almost all states of the country, having seen the condition of the poor from close quarters and felt in herself the woeful poverty of the people. She hears all sections of the people, particularly the poor and the weak, and draws schemes that provide them long-term benefits. She is always concerned about the farmers and the workers thinking that they are the backbone of the economy.

A crusader for corruption-free administration, she never gives credence to unscrupulous and unethical practices that are rampant in the society. She advocates for a mechanism that would ameliorate suffering and harassment of the poor people, values the laws of the land and supports stricter retribution for persons in authority who resort to unprincipled practices.

A person of high moral standing, Sonia never speaks ill of others. This aspect of her was evident when her opponents were making vitriolic remarks about her Italian origin. She never used offending words against anyone of them. She defends but not offends. She serves no self-interest but surely protects others'. She is neither holding any office of profit nor making enormous fortune for self. She has shunned fame and devotes herself completely for the country's development and the people's welfare. Being the President of the Congress Party by whose name people vote, she shouldn't remain an enigma. People who are interested to know about her will find this book a beacon of her qualities in public life. Some rare photographs have been used in the book to revive and preserve her old memories.

The book mainly offers her political accounts beginning with a brief description of her friendship with Rajiv Gandhi and roles in the Gandhi family. Accordingly, Chapter 1 is on her pre-marriage days, Chapter 2 on post-marriage days, Chapter 3 on entry into politics, Chapter 4 on parliamentarian role, Chapter 5 on election show-down and Chapter 6 on her role in governance.

Pre-marriage Days

1

BIRTH AND EDUCATION

Sonia Gandhi was born at Orbassano, a small town about 20 km from Turin, Italy on December 9, 1946. She is the second daughter of Stefano and Paola Mainos, the others are Anushka (elder) and Nadia (younger). Sonia's father named his daughters after Russian women who helped him when he was fighting in that country along with the Germans. She spent her adolescent days in Orbassano, being raised in a conservative Roman Catholic family. Her father was a building contractor. He died in 1988. Her mother still lives in Orbassano.

As the family was of conservative mindset, the three sisters studied in a Roman Catholic seminary about 15 km away from the town. According to Sonia's mates she was 'naughty'. Her schoolteacher could remember that she was well spirited and good at studies. Residents of Orbassano still remember her as a 'timid' but 'bright' girl. She used to play for hours drawing squares on the ground.

The school where Sonia studied used to organise various functions and she took part in most of them. She never insisted for better roles. Besides school functions, her other interest was playing football. She used to play football with boys and girls of the neighbourhood.

When grew up Sonia wanted to be a teacher but her father made up his mind that she pursue profession of an interpreter. So after completing her schooling it was decided that she be sent to Cambridge to study English. At the age of 18 she went to United Kingdom in 1965. She got admission to an English language school for foreign students and lived as a paying guest with an English family the arrangement of which was made by the school. Rajiv Gandhi, son of then Prime Minister Indira Gandhi, was also in the UK studying mechanical engineering in Cambridge's famous Trinity College.

The humbleness and decency of Rajiv always remained superb. Although a son of a prime minister he never visited luxurious hotels. His self-restrained nature surprised many of his close friends. They wondered how come a prime minister's son use to have meals in ordinary hotels?

As Sonia was away from home for the first time she was missing home terribly. She was also longing for Italian food immensely. She found in Cambridge a Greek restaurant called Varsity, where one could have something close to home food. She used to go there regularly for meals.

Sonia has recounted the circumstances vividly about how she first met Rajiv in her book *Rajiv*. By that account, a group of students used to frequent the restaurant. Among them Rajiv was something different. On many occasions he stood out in that group. He was remarkable in both looks and manners and was sober and calm, unlike the others. Comparatively he looked gentle, innocent, restrained and had charming smile.

RAJIV-SONIA FRIENDSHIP

Rajiv and Sonia first met at the Varsity restaurant. One day as Sonia was having lunch, a German friend of her who was fluent in Italian, walked upto her along with Rajiv whom she had often noticed. After the usual exchange of pleasantries, he introduced her to his friend Rajiv. When their eyes met for the first time, Sonia could feel her heart throbbing. As customary, they greeted each other. For Sonia it was love at first sight. She was a winsome young girl. Her charming beauty appealed Rajiv, so he too developed a liking for her. Later, dating and spending long hours in the restaurant blossomed into a deep love.

Those days Sonia had vague idea about India and thought that it existed somewhere in the world with its snakes, elephants and jungles, but exactly where it was, she didn't know. She found it out when a chance came from a school friend. "God, is that where India is—so far away at the other end!" This is what her first reaction was when she found the country on a map.

Both Rajiv and Sonia were enjoying their lives in Cambridge. As Rajiv was special among her friends she spent most of the time with him. Their time was passing happily. Now she no longer missed home as she used to do so earlier. Gradually they got to know each other better—spoke about themselves, their families and their aspirations. As Rajiv had already carved a niche in her heart, she found him quite sagacious.

The families of Sonia and Rajiv were of different backdrops. Sonia's father was a self-made man who worked hard to survive the post-war hardships. His laborious efforts bore fruit when his construction business flourished and led him moderately wealthy. He was known in his restricted provincial surroundings as Signor Maino, the owner of a building firm. About Rajiv's background, his family was known not only to the whole of India but to the world for the political role it had played in India's freedom struggle. It was Rajiv who told Sonia that his grandfather Jawaharlal Nehru died a year before and that his mother was a minister in the government.

Shedding hesitation Rajiv wrote to his mother about Sonia. As not bound by orthodox philosophy she expressed a wish to meet the girl on her coming visit to London on the occasion of Nehru Exhibition. Certainly, for Sonia the chance to meet Rajiv's mother was going to be a remarkable event. As for her own side, she couldn't muster enough courage to tell her parents about her feelings for Rajiv, who was to them not only a stranger but also a foreigner.

As Indira's arrival in London was approaching, the thought of meeting her terrified Sonia very much. A meeting was fixed and accordingly Rajiv drove Sonia down from Cambridge. As they reached London, Sonia became very panicked. She couldn't control herself thinking what Rajiv's mother would say. Rajiv tried to calm her down but it didn't help. At last he had to make an excuse and cancelled the scheduled meeting. Another day was fixed and this time Sonia made up her mind that she would behave herself. Sonia first met Rajiv's mother in her room at the High Commissioner's residence and drew a sigh of relief when she found that Rajiv's mother was perfectly a normal human being—warm and welcoming. Even she went out of her way to put Sonia at ease. She spoke to Sonia in French knowing that the girl was more fluent in it than in English. During their meeting Indira tried to know about Sonia and her studies and told her frankly that she needn't be frightened because she herself had been young, extremely shy and in love. In her short meeting she understood Sonia entirely. Sonia felt motherly touch from Rajiv's mother that day. Here it is how: In one of the anterooms Sonia changed into her evening dress, her high heel caught in the hem and tore a bit of it open. Indira, in calm fashion, took out a needle and black thread and proceeded to stitch up the hem. Sonia felt exactly the sort of thing her own mother would do. All the small doubts that had remained in her, immediately vanished.

Sonia remained in London for about two years, after which she returned home. Rajiv was having his flying lessons in London but both were in touch through letters. By this time their love grew profound. They wrote to each other regularly. She was worried that as her family was conservative and strict it may not be easy for her to get its acquiescence.

After getting his licence, Rajiv became very serious about his future. He travelled to Italy to talk to Sonia's father about his plans. Although her father had no doubts whatsoever about truthfulness of Rajiv, his only concerns were about his daughter thinking that she was too young to know about her mind, she couldn't possibly get used to life in India—such different people and custom. His aversion to marriage was because Rajiv being prime minister's son, she may not be able to adjust herself with the family. There was little possibility of her father permitting her even for a short holiday in India till she was of age.

Sonia showed enormous regards for her parents. When her father put one-year moratorium on their tryst thinking that it would lessen the intensity of love, she readily agreed. However, it was found that even after a year of separation Sonia and Rajiv still felt the same for each other. Now her father consented to her visiting to India 'to see for herself' so that she wouldn't blame him later for messing up her life. Realising that Rajiv and Sonia were deep in love Indira also felt that Sonia should come to India for a few months to see things for herself. As soon as Sonia turned 21, her father allowed her to travel to India.

It was a major victory for Sonia that she made her domineering father agree to the marriage who had great reservations for foreigners. At 21 she showed tremendous determination, courage, valour and fearlessness. It also reflected how deeply she was in love with Rajiv. Her decision later came out to be a feature of courage.

FIRST INDIA VISIT

On January 13, 1968 Sonia first set foot on India. It was the deep love that Sonia had for Rajiv made her travel to India all alone. Rajiv, Sanjay and his friend Amitabh Bachchan were at the Delhi airport to fetch her. The moment Sonia saw Rajiv, she was filled with a tremendous sense of relief. She was by Rajiv's side and felt that nothing and nobody would be able to separate them again. Sonia was staying with the Bachchans at their Wellingdon Crescent house and spent the days at 1, Safdarjung Road, until marriage took place.

Post-marriage Days

2

MARRIAGE

Indira wanted that Rajiv marry an Indian girl thinking she would care her better in old days. But when she understood very well that Rajiv and Sonia were very serious about their marriage plans, she gave her consent. Accordingly, Rajiv-Sonia engagement was held on January 26, 1968. Sonia's father didn't attend the marriage but her mother, sisters and maternal uncle Mario Predebon were present. A group photograph was taken shortly after the engagement. It marked the first time that Sonia appeared in public as the new member of the family. The marriage day was fixed for February 25, *Vasant Panchami* day, the day when Indira married Feroze Gandhi decades earlier. The commotion of the wedding preparation was soon in full swing: comings and goings, lists, invitations, tailors, etc. Sonia was in a daze for she had been at the centre of all these proceedings—terrified each time she wore a sari thinking that it would fall off, and wishing the hubbub to be over soon. Indira was very much against the pomp and wasteful display. She wanted the wedding to be a simple civil ceremony with two traditional rituals—the *jaimala* or the exchange of garlands and the chanting of *slokas* (hymns).

The day before the wedding, a *mehendi* ceremony was held at the Bachchans house. Here Sonia had an introduction to the Indian way of life. She was so impressed by their compassion that she looked upon Teji Bachchan as mother. On that occasion Sonia wore a simple *lehnga* (skirt) and *odhni* (veil), which were given to her mother-in-law by the *banjaras* (gypsies) of Andhra Pradesh and the traditional floral jewellery, *phoolon-ka-gehna* of Kashmiri brides.

The marriage was solemnized on the huge lawn of 1, Safdarjung Road. Indira supervised the arrangements. Her old friend Padmaja Naidu also helped her. The decoration was made tastefully with flowers and *alpana*. For the wedding, both Rajiv and Sonia observed family traditions in wearing *khadi*. Indira helped her in dressing the wedding sari. She looked elegant and beautiful in wedding dress. (Sonia wore a pink sari made from cotton that Nehru had spun while in prison. By the by it was the same sari that Indira wore for her wedding.) Rajiv wore *achkan* (coat) of off white silk and pink *safa* (turban).

Representatives of both the families witnessed the ceremony. Sonia's maternal uncle gave her away. Vijaya Laxmi Pandit, Nehru's sister; Prof. K.N. Kaul, Kamala Nehru's brother; Themina, Feroze's sister and Sonia's maternal uncle signed the register. When rings were exchanged, the assembly showered the rose petals. Then came the blessing by family members. The same evening, the couple moved into 1, Safdarjung Road. There was a reception at Hyderabad House the following evening.

Everything around Sonia was new and strange: the colours, the smell, the flavours and the people. Strangest of all were people's eyes—that gaze of curiosity, which followed her everywhere. It was an exasperating experience for her—the total lack of privacy, the compulsion to constantly check her and repress her feelings. She felt resentful and kept asking herself why those eyes were so insistent.

Sonia later discovered that this unnerving stare was not simply because she was a stranger and a foreigner, but because she was also a new member of the family, which had for years lived in the public eyes. Her immediate reaction was to retreat. Rajiv and his mother, both knew what shyness was, understood her feelings. Sonia was allowed to be herself and to find her own way of fitting into Rajiv's world. She began gradually to take interest in the running of the household. She started

Relatives of Gandhi family offering sweets to bride Sonia

learning Hindi, initially with a tutor at home and later at an institute. But she found it easier and more helpful to converse with the family and other members of the household. They generally spoke Hindi around the table. There would be lively conversation at the table: views exchanged and jokes traded.

The new addition to the Gandhi family became an instant favourite. Both Sonia and her mother-in-law became extremely fond of each other. According to Sonia, her mother-in-law was a delightful conversationalist—quick in observation and clear in description and her recollection of personalities and events of the Independence struggle could make history come alive.

Rajiv and Sonia settled into the tranquil togetherness they had been dreaming of. The newly married couple was leading lives away from limelight. Though the first son of the first political family, Rajiv avoided rough and tumble of politics. He thought it better to leave politics to mother and younger brother Sanjay. Rajiv was satisfied being an Indian Airlines pilot.

Initially Sonia was homesick. She would visit Italy with Rajiv every year and later every two years. Then once she thought that it was time to settle her mind in one country. As the roots of Rajiv are in India she preferred this country to be her motherland and it was through her heart that she loves it.

Rajiv had a Lambretta at first on which he and Sonia used to zip around, then a Jawa motorbike and later a Fiat. Rajiv's friends were from varied social backgrounds and were perfectly at ease with all of them. He was greatly liked by all for his readiness with a joke and a smile. So the couple's time passed nicely.

When Sonia was expecting her first baby she had to spend most of the nine months in bed. It was because she had a miscarriage a year before. Rajiv looked after her with utmost care and tenderness. When he was out flying, her mother-in-law would sit with her and do all she could to keep her spirit up. She took special delight in organising details of the coming grandchild's set of clothing. In 1970, their first child Rahul was born and second child Priyanka born a year later.

IDEAL HOUSEWIFE

Sonia gradually began to adjust herself in the Gandhi family and was discharging her role as a perfect housewife. As she was brought up in a conventional way she had no problem to bend herself accordingly in a joint family. Those who remained close to the family say that she was far more conventional, as seen in a Hindu wife. At times she used to go to market to buy vegetables and do the cooking in absence of the family cook. Many believe that she was never over-ambitious even though being a member of the country's first family.

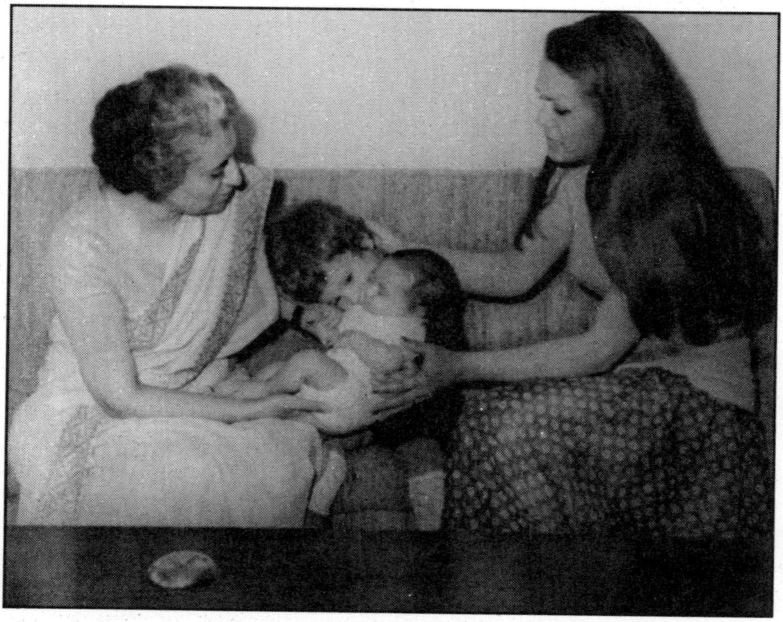

Sonia along with Indira enjoying a pleasant moment with her kids

During the troubled phase she tried to remain neutral and showed utmost loyalty to her mother-in-law and husband. Each member of the Gandhi household had an independent existence. Indira as Prime Minister had active life of her own. The family members always met over meals.

Being head of the family Indira was the central person. This position she got for her love and concern for all the family members. Despite the odds, Sonia felt more protective towards her mother-in-law whom she loved as her own mother. Sonia took particular interest in her necessities.

TRAGEDIES

Besides happy life in the Gandhi family, tragedies were lurking. These tragedies changed Sonia's course of life from time to time. The first tragedy descended on the family on June 23, 1980 when Sanjay (Rajiv's younger brother) died in a plane crash. Rajiv and Sonia were in Italy then. The incident was a shuttering blow for the family, particularly Indira.

Sanjay was politically very active. After his death an emotionally shattered Indira needed help. But Rajiv was least interested to enter into politics. Bowing to popular demand he, however, gave in. He resigned from the Indian Airlines in 1981 and joined politics, to give his mother a helping hand. It was a joint decision arrived at after long discussions with Sonia. She had her reservations but what could do in such circumstances?

Both Rajiv and Sonia were aware of the burdens of the power. They had apprehensions about the security of the family members. The situation in Punjab that time had escalated into a serious danger of the country's unity. Secessionist forces were gathering strength and brutal terrorist killings were mounting in numbers. After the Operation Blue Star, a shadow had entered into their lives. The trepidation was so high that once Indira spoke to Rajiv and Sonia about arrangements for her funeral.

Those apprehensions came true on October 31, 1984. Indira's own security guards assassinated her when she was walking from her home to the adjoining house. As the sound of the gunfire was heard, Sonia rushed out of her house. Seeing her mother-in-law in blood-ridden state she cried loudly. Immediately India was taken in a car to the All India Institute of Medical Sciences (AIIMS) and wheeled into the operating theatre. More than dozen doctors, including cardiologists and neuro-surgeons, began the operation to remove the bullets embedded in the abdomen, chest and thigh. Doctors declared her dead at 11 a.m. Rajiv, cutting short his West Bengal tour, flew back to Delhi.

On landing Rajiv rushed to the AIIMS to see his mother and came to know from the doctors that she was no more. Grief-ridden Rajiv was asked to become prime minister. In a fix for a moment he spoke to Sonia. Depressed Sonia virtually begged him not to accept the post. She was pleading with him saying that he would be killed as well. Rajiv held Sonia's hands, hugged her and tried to soothe her depression. Then he said he had no choice. Rajiv was sworn-in as Prime Minister in the evening.

Indira had a premonition about the attempt on her life. Addressing a public meeting in Orissa in the night earlier, she said in an emotional tone that even if she died in the service of nation, she would be proud of it. She said, "Every drop of my blood, I am sure, will contribute to the growth of this nation and to make it strong and dynamic." Indira was cremated four days later near Shanti Van, Nehru's mausoleum. As per her wish, her remains were mingled with the high mountains. The spot where she was assassinated is now a national pilgrimage.

Later both Rajiv and Sonia drafted identical and separately signed instructions for their children. Rajiv wrote: "In the event of my death as well as that of my wife, at or about the same time, at the same place and at different places, within or outside India, our bodies should be brought to Delhi and cremated together, in accordance with Hindu rites, in an open ground. In no circumstances should our bodies be burnt in a crematorium. According to our custom, our eldest child should light the pier. It is my wish that our ashes should be immersed into the Ganga at Triveni, Allahabad, where my ancestors' ashes have immersed."

From the day Sonia entered the Gandhi house as a young bride, through their happy and difficult times, Indira had been there, the pivot of their lives. Whatever happened—a problem to be solved, a squabble to be mediated, a special event to be celebrated—they would, each one of them, turn to her. She was there to guide, admonish and encourage them.

Indira loved Sonia very much. She perceived many qualities in her. This aspect of Indira was reflected in a letter that Sonia found after her death. It contained these words: "I am writing to you Sonia because you seem to be interested in the family and also because I see some glimpses of myself in you."

Sonia understood her new role and stood by her husband both when his popularity was at its zenith and when it ebbed. She used to accompany Rajiv whenever he toured Amethi constituency and used to nurse it for her husband. She also toured other parts of the country with her husband and mingled with people of different strata of the society. Though

Sonia accepted Rajiv's entry into politics, it took her some time to come to terms with it, particularly with the changes it was bringing to her life.

In the 1984 General elections, a wave of sympathy swept across the country. Rajiv came to power with unprecedented majority. As Prime Minister, he fully became involved in his work. Sonia and her children were aware of the magnitude of the threat against Rajiv after the violent death of Indira. When he was out, a slight delay in his schedule would automatically make them fear the worst.

Rajiv had a hectic schedule. The day would start with hundred of visitors on the lawns outside the Race Course Road office. In addition to all political and administrative work, there were ceremonial duties in which Sonia also participated—welcoming and seeing off visiting dignitaries and attending official functions.

Sonia also travelled with Rajiv to the remotest and poorest areas of India. She experienced the depth of feeling people had for him, how much he cared for them and the extent to which their love energized him. Wherever he came in contact with people, at the most glittering function or in the poorest home, she could sense that immediate change of excitement. It was more a response to his personal radiance than to the office he bore. It made little difference if it was a tribal village in the north, a town in the south, a hut in rural Punjab or a slum of Mumbai. Rajiv didn't belong to any group or caste or community.

Rajiv drove through most villages and towns in jeep. Whenever he saw people waiting, he would stop. Sonia had seen that if they were delayed, people would remain stand-by patiently, to see Rajiv and to talk to him. Rajiv was so favourite to them that late at night, in a far off area, an old lantern would be lifted close to his face. They wanted Rajiv to meet their families, to name their newborn babies, to bless their young couple. He sometimes shared their meagre meals, comforted them, asked them questions and listened attentively to their simple and frank description of hardships.

Rajiv and Sonia with villagers near Agra

It was this direct contact with the people and looking at problems from their viewpoint that reinforced Rajiv's determination to bring in the changes and innovations he knew were needed. He was young and full of energy and had a vision for the country. He had a dream to take the country to the 21st century with a bang. Every step toward that goal brought him joy and satisfaction.

Then came the 1989 General Elections. The right and left wing parties joined hands forming a political platform with one aim that is removal of Rajiv. His campaign was on his Government's achievements. He brought new policies, new initiatives. The Government managed economic crisis very efficiently. Many of the conflicts it inherited had been resolved. The Opposition campaign was about slander and abuse of Rajiv and his family.

As the election results were out, it became clear that the Congress party couldn't form a government on its own. Even though the party won largest number of seats, Rajiv resigned from Prime Minister's post. His dream got shuttered mid-way. He was very disappointed that the target he set to achieve couldn't be accomplished.

There had been constant threats to his life from the extremist groups. Two attempts were already made earlier on his life—one on October 2, 1986 at Rajghat and another on July 30, 1987 in Colombo. By 1989, there were a dozen major terrorist outfits. For each one of them Rajiv and his family members were the targets. The new governments were well aware of the threat perception that Rajiv had been with, yet they withdrew specialised security cover and replaced it with a force not trained for this specific task. Everyday brought new and glaring examples of how lightly Rajiv's security was viewed and how carelessly it was handled. Once Rahul accompanied his father on a tour to Bihar and was appalled to witness the lack of elementary security around his father. Before going back to America he told his mother that if something were not done about it, he would have to come home soon for his father's funeral.

Neither of the two successor governments lasted. It was during the campaigning of the 1991 General Elections, tragedy struck again. Just when it appeared that Rajiv was on a comeback trail, he was brutally assassinated by the LTTE (Liberation Tigers of Tamil Eelam) human bomb at an election rally at Seriperimbudur in Tamil Nadu. According to his wish, his body was brought to Delhi and cremated in an open ground adjacent to his mother's mausoleum.

The assassination of her husband shattered Sonia tremendously. What she feared had come true. The shock she received remained with her for quite a long time. The happiness of her life came to a dead-end.

SOLITARY LIFE

After husband's death, Sonia led a life of recluse for almost six years. She was greatly worried about the future of her children. The fear of terror affected their schooling. Her children had grown up. Besides their education, the safety and security were her main concern. She was her own councillor at that stage and all decisions had to be taken by her only, guided as much by intuition as by logic and force of circumstances. By that time she had developed tremendous liking for the country. Having travelled throughout the length and breadth of the country, she had seen how people look to the Gandhi family. This very thought made her finally decide to remain in India, accepting it as her permanent abode.

Sonia was leaving a solitary life. Only a few persons with whom she had acquaintances were allowed to visit her residence. She only made brief appearances at some official functions. During this time she had been receiving requests to join politics but she spurned all of them.

As Sonia made up her mind to remain in India, she adapted herself to Indian culture very quickly. Now she started to familiarise well with Indian custom, culture and cuisine. Shedding her fluttering skirt, she moulded completely to the Indian tradition. She switched over to India's most favoured dress sari and blouse. The way she drapes herself, it gives her ideal Indian look. So perfectly she wears it that no one can say she is an Italian.

Sonia moulds herself so nicely that she can be fit under any situation. When she visits remote villages, the way she mixes up with the villagers, particularly women, it is hard to believe that a dignified personality can do that. She never likes showy dress. Printed sari is her ideal choice. She has also changed her hair-do. The silky and wavy hair is passé, now she dons plait or round tress.

Sonia by now learnt the Hindi language very well and could communicate with people easily. Priyanka helped her brush up on Hindi vocabulary. Slowly and steadily she grasped the language and could talk with anyone without any difficulty. She used to take part in various religious functions freely.

Though it is desired that everyone know the national language well but as India is a multi-lingual country, people prefer to talk in their mother tongue. Hindi is taught in non-Hindi belt schools up to class VIII. Many Indians are not good in reading, writing or speaking the language. It is not the criterion to disqualify anybody from enjoying governmental benefits or occupying important constitutional position.

Former Prime Minister H.D. Deve Gowda knew little Hindi before he moved to Delhi to head the United Front Government. After becoming Prime Minister, he took regular Hindi coaching to converse and even to attempt to speak a few words at public platforms.

SPECIAL INTEREST

During hectic activity as housewife Sonia joined National Museum where she pursued varied interest in Indian contemporary classical and tribal art, handloom and handicraft, oil painting and their conservation. She is a perfectionist. No matter what she picks up, the work has to be done to perfection. It is only when something is well done that she is satisfied.

Sonia has authored two books entitled *Rajiv* and *Rajiv's World* and edited *Freedom's Daughter* and *Two Alone, Two Together* (on the letters exchanged between Jawaharlal Nehru and Indira Gandhi from 1922 to 1964).

Entry Into Politics

3

POLITICAL BAPTISM

Sonia had a great aversion to politics. When Indira and Rajiv were alive, Sonia showed indifference to power and glory. There was not a single instance of Sonia attending any public function or holding any public office during her powerful mother-in-law's tenure as prime minister. After Rajiv became Prime Minister, then also she maintained her detachment from public life and office. She could have any public office for the asking but never showed any interest for it. After her husband's death, she still showed no such interest. For her dislike to politics she spurned every request of the Congress leaders to enter into it for long seven years. She even opposed Rajiv tooth and nail from entering it. The aversion was so great that Sonia once threatened to divorce Rajiv if did so. Rajiv later explained this aversion saying, "Sonia felt she would be losing me."

The Congress leaders continued their appeal to her to join politics. They felt that being a member of the Nehru-Gandhi family she would be an asset for the party. When she refused the appeal just after her husband's assassination, the party installed veteran leader P.V. Narasimha Rao as party chief and subsequently as prime minister. His government was more or less stable, though the name of the party was sullied under him as never before over the incident of Babri mosque demolition.

When Rao demitted office, Sonia again got the offer to become Congress chief. Then also she refused to accept the post. After her refusal, veteran Congressman Sitaram Kesri became the party President. Kesri, however, couldn't keep the Congress leaders united. The party started sinking under him as it was losing elections and the partymen were drifting away to either join another party or form a new party (Mamata Banerjee formed Trinamool Congress in 1997). This was the reason the Congress leaders were putting constant pressure on Sonia to take the party's command.

Many Congress leaders were unhappy with Kesri's style of functioning. They began to term him as 'liability' for the party. Many leaders, namely Mani Shankar Aiyar, Suresh Kalmadi, Buta Singh, Aslam Sher Khan left the party and many more were willing to leave it. Senior leaders again urged Sonia, to name a few Jitenrdra Prasada, Vijay Bhaskar Reddy, Arjun Singh, K. Karunakaran, Sharad Pawar, to take the party's command. The young Turks didn't lag behind. Leaders such as Ahmed Patel, Vayalar Ravi, Kamal Nath, Ashok Gehlot were repeatedly asking her to play active role in the party. They feared that under Kesri's leadership, the party couldn't be saved from its declining trend.

After much persuasion, at the end of 1997 as the nation was going for General elections, Sonia agreed to campaign for the party. Her first meeting was at Seriperimbudur. She addressed many election meetings. As a result of her campaigning the party won many seats that were quite unexpected. Congress leaders credited her for this.

Sonia remained away from politics up to 1998. Party leaders continued their appeal, asking her to become leader of the party. Kesri also announced that he would step down in favour of her. The leaders almost lost patience. Those close to Sonia went to her residence and made their intention clear. It was a coup type of situation. The leaders wanted Kesri to immediately step down, but he was not prepared for that. The situation came to such a pass that at last she deemed it proper to give acquiescence. The Congress Working Committee (CWC) met and approved Sonia's name. It was on March 14 that the Congress leaders replaced Kesri's nameplate with Sonia's.

BECOMES CONGRESS CHIEF

On April 6, 1998 the All India Congress Committee (AICC) ratified Sonia's appointment as President of the organisation. She became the third woman of foreign origin to hold the prestigious post after Annie Besant and Neli Sengupta and the fifth from the Nehru family—the other fours were Motilal Nehru, Jawaharlal Nehru, Indira Gandhi and Rajiv Gandhi. She became primary member of the party just months before the Kolkata plenary in August 1997.

It was a matter of great rejoicing for the Congress leaders that party's responsibility had been conferred upon competent Sonia. They believed that under her efficient leadership a political regeneration would develop and the country march towards path of progress.

As Sonia became President of the Congress, there prevailed unity in the party. She also took steps to revamp the organisation. But more than a year later she had to face revolt from some of the party leaders who themselves repeatedly requested her to take plunge into politics. Three party leaders—Sharad Pawar, P.A. Sangma and Tariq Anwar—waged an open revolt against Sonia on the issue of her foreign origin. They became critical of the Congress for failing to get a qualified Indian for its President and for projecting her as prime ministerial candidate.

To convey resentment, the trio later submitted their resignations to her. Realising that she was the cause of the turmoil in the party, she too conveyed to the CWC members her decision to stay away. However, the CWC rejected her resignation and decided to remain solidly behind her. When the CWC members called on her, she told them that she was deeply hurt by the attitude of some party leaders about her foreign origin.

Despite several attempts, the rebels couldn't be persuaded to withdraw their resignations. In another meeting, the CWC decided to expel the rebels for violating party discipline. The CWC members continued to put pressure on her to reconsider her decision. Fully knowing that she was indispensable for the party, she decided to take back her resignation.

Sonia believes in true democracy. In 1999 she was elected party President first time through the process of ballot. Veteran Congress leader Jitendra Prasada contested against her. But it was a one-sided fight from the word 'go'. After the Congress party regained power at the Centre in 2004, election was again held for party President. In 2005 she was again elected President second time by overwhelming support. Although the election schedule was announced, no leader came forward to contest the post, as they knew that it was she who would be the ideal choice. Presumably she was declared re-elected unopposed. The five-member bench of the election committee declared Sonia's unanimous election after scrutiny of the nomination papers, all of which were in her favour. Out of the total 100 nomination papers, 97 were found valid. The official announcement was only a matter of formality as no nomination was filed against her.

Under Sonia's able leadership, the Congress party was in power in 15 states in just six years. Even her detractors commend her for role in holding the party together. However, she maintains that she is "no saviour" of the party.

With humble submission Sonia said, "I am grateful to the workers and leaders for having reposed faith in me. Despite the fact that we have come to power after eight years and leading a coalition government we have to be alert and to work relentlessly to strengthen the organisation.

Sonia took over the reins of the party when it was on the verge of crumbling. Many people, not knowledgeable about the realities of the party, often argue that the number of Members of Parliament during Kesri's leadership was more as compared to Sonia's time. Although the argument seems to be correct, the truth is that during Kesri's tenure the morale of the workers was so low that if it had not been Sonia's entry into politics, the Congress would have been reduced to double-digit figures. The evidence of the damage that was caused to the party in several states during the tenures of Rao and Kesri were there as many party activists later admitted how they attempted to rebuild the party from scrap.

The Nehru dynasty is indispensable for the Congress. It has led the Congress and the country for 37 post-Independence years out of 42, with breaks only in 1964-66 (Lal Bahadur Shastri) and 1977-1980 (Morarji Desai of Janata Party). When non-Congress governments ruled the country, people had little hope from them and remained confused over governments' stability. Sonia stepped into politics when the party was in Opposition. It was really an uphill task for her to revive the party because first, she was a political novice and second, she was of foreign origin.

Sonia persevered continuously for the party's success. At the time of elections she did maximum campaigning. First came the success in Delhi, Madhya Pradesh and Rajasthan in 1998. In later years the party won several elections. The political pundits earlier had given up hope about the future of the Congress party but she had not only revived it but also brought it to power in three states that were ruled by the BJP. Slowly and surely more than half the country came to the party's fold. Obviously with such a success she has proved that she is not an average politician. Under her leadership, the party is consolidating on its lost base. In Maharashtra, several prominent Shiv Sena leaders have joined the party. In Karnataka also same thing happened. The party under her continues to be the largest political formation in the country.

Along with the success were the challenges. Sonia had to face the onslaught of the adversaries over her foreign origin. The three rebel leaders had formed a separate entity, the Nationalist Congress Party (NCP). They made her foreign origin main plank during election campaigns. However, the foreigner issue remained buried ever since the Supreme Court gave its verdict on this matter. The controversy over her origin also went to the back burner with Pawar relenting. He said at the NCP conclave in Mumbai, "Our ego had grown taller than our height."

The trio were repeatedly saying that Sonia couldn't be elected as prime minister because of her foreign origin. Sonia, however, lashed out at Pawar for raising doubts about her identity and nationality. In 2002 Pawar's NCP delinked the issue of Sonia's origin. NCP's Praful Patel admitted that there was no constitutional, legal or democratic bar to her possible claim to prime ministership. His argument against such a claim was that it was a matter of sentiment. "If majority of the people want her to be at that post, what we can do," he said.

As President of the party, Sonia had generated a wave of enthusiasm among the leaders and cadres. With her family background as well as on her personal capacity, she rejuvenated the party that had been bereft of a charismatic leader. She also resurrected the Nehru-Gandhi ideology, thus adding a dynamic dimension to its affairs. She stands for highest ideals of the party, which are secularism and progress.

Sonia is now a matured politician. Her guidance and ability in cobbling the coalition and running its government successfully are the shining examples of her maturity. Her political maturity can be gauged from the fact that she alone was instrumental in shaping the coalition and now takes no pains in resolving differences that appears between the Congress party and the supporting partners in the course of running the government.

PERSONALITY

Sonia's dignified behaviour, enigmatic image and towering personality fascinate all. She is a principled person and knows very well her duty towards one and all. She also has a helpful disposition. She believes in simplicity and is a strong votaress of austerity. She is for full implementation of what has been preached.

Sonia's real power is her acceptability as a leader by the Congressmen. With her courteous behaviour, sophisticated persona and refined deportment, she has become persona grata to them. By her kind and compassioned nature plus subtle temperament, she has won the hearts of crores of people—rich and poor alike. Her popularity increased by leaps and bounds and soon became a household name all over the country.

On her part, Sonia has fully dedicated herself to the service of the Congress party and the people. Crave for pelf and power never overpowered her earnest desire to work for the betterment of the downtrodden. She has expounded the dogma—purity in thought, politeness in speech and active in action. She is also a great mediator—intervenes promptly when workers' or weaker sections' interests are affected.

Sonia spends most of the time in thinking of the welfare of the people. She is always prepared to assist people in every way she can and this comes out of her sincere love for them. There is no selfishness at all. She never thinks what she can get from others but thinks what she can give to them. To ameliorate the sufferings of the poor and the needy, she holds *durbar* at her residence. Many disgruntled soles come to her for help.

The two persons on whom Sonia depends most for emotional supports are Rahul and Priyanka. When a very important decision is to be taken she consults only with them. Even the close coteries are not told about such decisions. Although Priyanka is busy with her kids, she speaks to her mother several times in a day. Sonia's emergence into the political arena and her evolving as a political persona were all done with Rahul and Priyanka's approval.

Congress leaders generally don't have access to close family interactions. In fact, Sonia is such a reticent person that she will not reveal her feelings to even close friends. She has metamorphosed to a woman of greater determination. Shedding shyness she has emerged as a much more combative woman. Earlier she was not willing to come out from her private world, now she has bestowed herself fully to public service—remaining busy the whole day meeting people and holding consultations.

ABLE LEADER

Several assembly results have proved that Sonia is providing good leadership to the party. The opponents always fear about her masterstroke because she knows the art of political manoeuvring by which she can take the wind out of the opponents' sails.

Besides showing mettle on political field, she has basic compassionate attitude. She has the caring quality and feels bad when innocent people become victims of mischievous acts perpetrated by others. Some of the common traits that strike one's mind are that she shows promptness in mitigating the sufferings of the people who are affected by some way or the other. Her visits to Varanasi and Mumbai in the wake of serial blasts or to Meerut when a major fire tore through a consumer goods fair in which more than 60 people got burnt and over 120 injured or her meeting with the quake-affected people of Jammu and Kashmir tell it all. She thinks for well-being of others, particularly the poor and the women. For their benefit several laws have been enacted under her initiative. Her other remarkable features are right attitude and credibility.

Sonia's approach is constructive and has foresightedness. Her goals do not end up in a utopia. She visualises the future precisely. She has faith in subordinates and delegates responsibilities to them and watch them perform well. She has set an example that is unmatched.

Sonia doesn't like publicity for herself. Several times she urged the partymen to desist from this. Her observation at the AICC meeting held in New Delhi in 2004 is a pointer to this effect. When chants of *Sonia Gandhi Zindabad* rent the air she pointed out that had the speakers concentrated less on praising her, they could have come up with something substantive. At Hyderabad plenary also she strongly disapproved of her eulogisation and asked partymen not to praise her too much. "There is no need to speak too much about me," she said.

Sonia's speech is remarkable for simplicity and forcefulness. Whatever she says, it comes from her heart. The following one-liner best substantiates the observation: *Desh aur samaj ke vikas mein Kendra ki bhumika kafi badi hai. Jab tak hum Kendra mein shashan nahi karenge, desh ka vikas sambhav nahin hai* (The government has a key role to perform in transforming society. Till such time as the Congress does not come to power at the Centre, no proper development can take place). This is how she convinced people.

Sonia has the unique ability to keep the flock together and put down rebellion. She doesn't hesitate to use her authority in the party. Sometimes a situation comes when a tricky problem is to be solved or more than one claimant vie for a position. Then she has the final say. No one in the party can muster courage to go against her decision.

The Congress is a democratic party and to maintain discipline within the party Sonia has advised the partymen to use appropriate fora to vent their grievances. She has always been able to overcome threats from other parties but it came to the notice that party leaders sometimes criticise their own government. Such things cause her embarrassment. According to her, the 'enemy within' is more destructive than the 'enemy outside'. She laments that the partymen talk against own government. When the party loses election the partymen make irresponsible statement, which harms the spirit of the cadres. She advised the party workers to desist from factional feuds and instead strengthen the organisation through united efforts.

Sonia urged the workers that it was the responsibility of everybody to keep the monumental heritage intact. "We should shun a narrow-minded approach and broaden our vision and mindset. Infighting will weaken the party so the workers should take a pledge to work shoulder to shoulder." She believes that only Congress can deliver unselfish service to the poor.

Parliamentary Life

4

BECOMES AN MP

In 1999 Sonia first stepped into parliamentary life winning election from the Amethi Lok Sabha constituency. She subsequently became Leader of the Opposition. It took her some time to familiarise herself with the functioning of the Parliament. As she used to talk in Hindi at home there was no problem whatsoever for her to communicate with other members in the House. She shed inhibitions quickly and began to raise issues concerning the masses.

The various positions Sonia held so far, she excelled in all. As Leader of the Congress Parliamentary Party (CPP), she enjoyed the confidence of all the MPs and as Opposition leader, she brought censure motions against the Vajpayee Government quite skilfully. The Rs. 15 crore relief package for Gujarat announced by the Government was an indication of the success of the censure motion.

As Opposition leader Sonia discharged her role with great responsibility. She raised many crucial issues in the Lok Sabha that were of immense importance. The party brought many motions against the Vajpayee Government. One important motion was in August, 2000 when its member Priya Ranjan Dasmunshi moved it on the need to appoint a commission of inquiry into the Amarnath killings. The motion was defeated by a voice vote. During the Ayodhya controversy, Sonia did not remain silent. She again brought motion in December the same year. Party member Jaipal Reddy demanded that Prime Minister Atal Behari Vajpayee drop L.K. Advani, M.M. Joshi and Uma Bharti from the Government for their involvement in the Babri Masjid demolition case and disapproved Vajpayee's stand to exonerate them. However, only 179 members voted in favour of the motion while 291 members negated it. A censure motion in April, 2002 discussed the Gujarat situation. The motion couldn't destabilise the regime but it definitely undermined the coalition Government's stability.

Sonia cornered Vajpayee Government whenever any scam surfaced. She brought 'no confidence' motion against the Government in August 2003 with several scam charges. As the countdown began for the motion, the party chalked out its strategy to raise issues highlighting the 'failures' of the Government on various fronts. The high level political affairs committee, billed as the 'Super CWC' of the party, decided the issues such as failure on internal security, financial crisis, farmers' plight, foreign policy front etc. Other issues like petroleum scam, telecom scam, UTI scam, coffin scam, PAC report on defence purchases during Kargil war, misuse of the CBI were also short-listed. On August 20 the House debated the motion. So strong was the verbal attack that even Advani and Fernandes, known for their exceptional debating ability, seemed to be short on reason. She delivered speech for an hour. Instead of responding to the questions she raised, Vajpayee, Advani and Fernandes focused on her language and style. What they meant to say was that her case did not do India proud.

The Congress criticised the Vajpayee Government for not fulfilling the promises made to the public about generation of one crore employment each year. The Government, however, painted a rosy picture about growing employment opportunities saying that due to creation of job openings in information technology, tourism, financial services among others, employment sector had shown an upward trend during the last several years.

Vajpayee made a face-saving argument saying that due to globalisation and economic liberalisation, the employment opportunities in the older types of enterprises might have been reduced. He admitted that unemployment across the country remained a huge problem but said the Government was committed to create employment opportunities for one crore people per year.

Sonia never hesitated to raise issues that were detrimental to the interest of the common people. She even charged Vajpayee whenever she found some wrong doings on the part of his Government. On many occasions her charges caused embarrassment to the Government. The issues concerning national security, communal harmony and public welfare always remained uppermost in her mind. Many times she felt that what Vajpayee said one day, he deviated from it later. On this she once questioned his rational thinking.

Sonia accused the BJP leadership of tending to lose its 'balance of mind' each time she presented its real face to the people. She did not name Vajpayee, but the reference was very much clear. She even questioned the new anti-terror law, which was passed on the strength of a technical majority by making both the Houses sit together.

Sonia remained unwavering in her criticism of Vajpayee's Gujarat visit in 2002 and termed the bloodbath after the Godhra train fire as an indelible 'blot' on the nation's secular fabric. Sonia accused Vajpayee of disregarding the sensitivities of Gujarat's riot victims by keeping Chief Minister Narendra Modi in toe all through his visit to the state. In fact, Vajpayee's tour of Gujarat came in handy for her, who got back at him for his outburst against her at Parliament's joint sitting.

Sonia paid a day-long visit to the strife-torn Gujarat as a member of the All-party Delegation and listened to the plight of the victims. She said, "The Central Government sees nothing wrong in a chief minister whose law and order administration is so infested by the politics of communalism that it victimises officials who take a courageous stand against communal violence." She also sat on a *dharna* at Rajghat demanding dismissal of Modi government.

The saffron associates came to their senses after a long silence. NDA Convenor George Fernandes decided belatedly to bring a peace march after mutely watching the turmoil. The reason for bringing out such a march was that the liberal sections among the Hindus became outrageous due to prolong disorder. The business community was also unhappy over the continuing violence. Fernandes led the march presumably because if a leader of the BJP, which was widely suspected to be behind the pogrom, led the procession it would have demeaned its importance.

It may be possible that the NDA Convenor was chosen to do the needful because he never took rigid stand on the need to remove the Chief Minister. His march wasn't a notable success. In fact, it was quickly followed by more violence, suggesting that such belated effort served no purpose.

On Kargil issue Sonia took Vajpayee Government to task. Cornering the Vajpayee Government she said, "We have seen the patriotism of the BJP, which Government was sleeping while the enemy entered the country. Those who cannot ensure the security of the country have no business to stay in power even for a minute." On armsgate and coffingate she criticised the Government saying, "The episode has opened the eyes of the people to the fact that corruption has penetrated every level in the Government like cancer."

On Indo-Pak summit Sonia said, "With each passing day the fallout of the much-published Indo-Pak summit at Agra was becoming messier and confusing. Right from the word 'go' the summit had gone on the wrong track." On Parliament attack she flayed the Vajpayee Government thus: "I hope the Government will look into and share with the nation the reasons why the terrorists could make all preparations unhindered and literally knocked at the doors of our Parliament House, despite prior information...."

If one compared Vajpayee's speech with Sonia's, he wouldn't say that she came second best. Many discount the obsession with her as an orator. People were convinced by her greater touch with reality. She is also concerned about *kisans* and *mazdoors*. This aspect of her can be understood when she said: "When I talk about *kisans* and *mazdoors*, my opponents are only interested in attacking me personally". Earlier, one couldn't imagine her talking about *kisans* and *mazdoors*. This shows how Sonia has wider comprehension about the domestic affairs and that as Opposition leader she cannot remain silent about the plight of the lower sections of the society.

It is worthy of mentioning that the Leader of the Opposition is a public office carrying the rank of a cabinet minister. The Government consults the Opposition leader on major policy matters.

IDEOLOGY AND FAITH

The Congress vision is rooted in the idea of one nation with a unique diversity of people's creeds and cultures. Country's core values have always been its liberal mind and its tradition of tolerance. The politics of hate is alien to its civilization. The party strives to bring advancement and well-being of the people through constitutional means.

As Congress President, Sonia fully understands the ideology and values that the party stands for. She plays clean politics and believes in transparency, not in hidden agenda. She is of the view that once elected, the government must work for the betterment of the people. That is why whatever her party promises to the electorate, she whole-heartedly tries to keep them.

The Congress functions on certain basic values like unity of the people, no division on caste or regional lines, rapid economic development, independent foreign policy, commitment to equality and social justice and improvement in the quality of the lives of the people. It is for involvement of all sections of the people in the nation building.

The Congress is the only party that has wider social base and large reach—among the poor farmers, the working people, the suppressed castes, the women, the religious, ethnic and linguistic minorities as well as among the middle class and higher social strata. The party is constantly fighting to preserve and maintain democratic and social values.

Sonia receives a memorandum from the minority community

Sonia believes in true secularism and emulates Rajiv's assertion made in his first address to the nation from the ramparts of Red Fort that "secularism is bedrock of our nationhood". If there is anything where Sonia has taken an uncompromising line, it is communalism and it is this stand that she emerged triumphant in many elections.

Sonia runs the Congress party on this very basis. She knows very well that if the party deviates from the secular path, it would be impossible to keep the nation united. The party's secular credential has been tested over the years. Even other political parties endorse this. Those parties, which believe in similar creed, join hands with the Congress to take on the communal forces.

The Nehru-Gandhi dynasty believes in genuine secularism. More than anything else, it is this legacy that attracts the liberal intelligentsia. Sonia is able to bring together secular forces on one side to take on the communal forces. The Left parties also believe that the Congress is secular by the core and join hands with it in fighting communal forces.

The Opposition party charged that Sonia follows soft *Hindutva*. Criticising the BJP for launching malicious propaganda, the Congress chief said she didn't follow soft *Hindutva*. "If I go to Kamakhya temple in Guwahati as I have been doing for many years, why should I be accused of soft *Hindutva*? If I visit Dargah and meet Muslim clerics, why should I be accused of appeasement? These are labels that have no meeting points", she said.

Sonia's contribution towards maintaining peace and harmony is immense. After the Congress formed Government at the Centre under her leadership, the fear of Godhra type of pogrom has vanished from the minds of minorities. Any assault on the values of tolerance, secularism and plurality makes her very sad.

Sonia considers that the Congress is the only party that guarantees for all-inclusive pluralistic society. She also maintains her pro-plurality attitude ever since she became party President. She is for strict adherence to pluralistic society. According to her own perception India can realise her aspirations for global leadership if it remains all-inclusive at home.

If there is one thing where Sonia has uncompromising line, it is communalism. She has firm resolve to fight against communalism. Whenever a communal disturbance is reported, she remains perturbed. She understands that riots only cause bitterness among the communities and give rise to conflicts. She strongly believes in the concept of one big family.

Sonia doesn't follow a particular religion but have faith in all. As teenager, she used to visit church regularly. Her intention to visit church declined as she grew up. At Cambridge she rarely attended church service. Here too she is not regular in visiting the church, but doesn't miss Christmas Mass. She has adopted the religion of her husband that is Hindu and wishes that her last rites be performed according to the Hindu ritual.

In her initial years in the Gandhi family Sonia knew many things about faith from her mother-in-law. On several occasions her mother-in-law accompanied her whenever she visited famous shrines in the country. Her husband also took her along when he visited renowned religious places. She has already visited some of the country's famous temples—from Kamakhya Temple in Assam to Ambaji Temple in Gujarat and Harmandar Sahib Temple in Amritsar to Tirupati Temple in Andhra Pradesh—to seek blessings. Whenever she visits religious places she shows great respect to them and pays obeisance as an ardent devotee. On invitation she participates in religious functions of different faiths.

Sonia best realises that without secular credential, India cannot survive. She is secularist in thought as well as in action. She has great respect for all religions and fully understands that friendship and goodwill among different faiths are the essential conditions for peace in the country. That is why she has embodied principles like spirit of sacrifice, unity and diversity.

Sonia is a strong believer in democratic values and has special honour for those who come through the system. Based on this ideal, she declared after becoming party President for the second time that there would be election for the CWC posts. Reacting to her such intentions, several state party units passed resolutions asking her to nominate CWC members instead of holding formal elections. But she reiterated the same intention even at the Chandigarh conclave. "I am always in favour of democratic methods. I do believe elections are preferable," she said. This shows her commitment to the ideals of parliamentary democracy.

FOREIGN ORIGIN

As soon as Sonia entered into politics, her foreign origin became a talking point for the rival parties. After coming to power, the BJP-led NDA Government set up a Constitution review committee, which among other things was to see propriety to bar a person of foreign origin from holding top constitutional post. However, when the committee failed to arrive at a consensus, Sangma, who was in the panel, came out of it. Prior to the General elections he said Sonia's foreign origin was still the main issue before the people who couldn't accept her as the prime minister of the country.

The BJP leadership felt that Sonia's foreign origin was the only issue by which her popularity could be checked. So the party made her origin an issue at election campaign and talked about it at every platform. The BJP leaders tried to mould public opinion against her using it as a weapon.

The campaign was politically motivated. Moreover, the irony was that those who raised her foreign origin were the same people who did nothing against the foreign rulers when they actually remained here. In other words, their ideology had nothing do with patriotism. It was partisan politics born out of dissatisfaction. It seemed there was an attempt to divert the attention of the people from infightings going on within the NDA Government.

The question of Sonia's foreign origin came off and on because the leaders of the rival parties were greatly concerned about her increasing popularity. They feared that in near future she certainly would make it to the prime minister's post. To counter such a possibility, they used every opportunity to influence the electorate. Their argument was that no self-respecting nation could have a person of foreign origin in top constitutional office. They believed that a head of state/government must be an ideal person, he/she must be able to lay down agenda, should have an ideology, be able to give direction for making policy and tackle serious issues—ranging from foreign affairs to economic.

The leaders of the rival parties began to doubt Sonia's ability to deal with various burning issues facing the country. They thought that she had no comprehension and understanding about these issues. This lack of understanding emanated from the fact that she didn't born in India and had no sufficient familiarity with the country and its system of governance. They also had doubt about her commitment towards the country.

The BJP viewed it reprehensible that the Congress chose Sonia for the top post not because of any intrinsic merit but by virtue of her marriage into the Gandhi family. This in itself was an admission that the Congress couldn't look outside the dynasty. The party even questioned as to why she took long years to become a citizen of the country. (She adopted Indian citizenship in 1983)

On Sonia's foreign origin issue, the Congress alleged that by launching personal attack on her, the BJP broke all norms of decency—rationally or morally. The Congress accused that as ethical code of conduct remained constantly alien to the BJP, its only aim seemed to seize power at all cost.

The BJP's denouncement of Christianity had become symbolized in its prime target Sonia. Through attack on her it was targeting two birds with one stone—to pull down a powerful claimant to the prime minister's office and personifying in her all minorities in general and the Christians in particular.

The country's Constitution doesn't bar anybody from holding high office on citizenship ground. The Supreme Court settled the matter once and for all when it categorically ruled that the foreign origin couldn't be a disqualification for holding a constitutional position. This means, Sonia's birth couldn't be invoked to keep her out of office. So as far as legal dimension goes, there remained absolutely no room for ambiguity in this regard.

In a landmark judgement, the Supreme Court made it clear in 2001 that Sonia is a citizen of India. Rejecting a petitioner's argument that she was an Italian national and a citizen of Italy, the Court held that she acquired Indian citizenship in 1983 under section 5(1)(c) of the Indian Citizenship Act on the ground of having married an Indian citizen, so her citizenship is very much valid.

About five years later the Supreme Court rejected another petition filed by some practising advocates of Varanasi against Sonia. The petitioners challenged her election to the Lok Sabha on the grounds that she still owed allegiance to Italy and hence was not a citizen of India. They alleged that in her affidavit filed before the Returning Officer at the time of filing nomination papers in 2004, she mentioned owning of a house in Italy that she inherited from her ancestors, which amounted to having allegiance to a foreign state and continued to be citizen of Italy. They argued that according to the Constitution of Italy, a person born there can't become citizen of another country and hence she was not an Indian citizen. They further contended that who is not citizen of India can neither become voter nor can contest election and hence not only the election of her liable to be set aside but also be debarred from contesting elections in future. The Court dismissed the petition on frivolous ground.

India is a great country and throughout the history the Indians have accepted many foreigners, cultures and faiths. There are a few fundamentalists who go against this ethos but most people are generous and large hearted. Many of them have accepted Sonia as their leader. Despite the apex court's ruling, Sonia's foreign origin issue swayed some section of the people, particularly the urban middle class. In the minds of the common people there was no such anxiety.

Sonia did nothing wrong that could politically distinguish her from other politicians. The foreign origin was the only issue that set her apart from the others. That was the reason her critics harped time and again on her Italian parentage.

One senior BJP leader launched a scathing attack on the Congress and targeted Sonia on her foreign origin. At a public meeting in Assam in 2002 he said, "We have nothing to comment on the Congress selecting Sonia as the party chief. But when it comes to who will be the country's prime minister, the people will decide, not the Congress." He further said, "As Parliamentarian she not once in the four years of the BJP rule ask a question to Vajpayee. This is the state of the leader of the Opposition. She needs someone to write her the questions. She just can't think on her own and has no ability to play the role of Opposition leader and under such circumstances how can she even dream of becoming the nation's prime minister."

Reacting to his allegations, Assam Chief Minister Tarun Gogoi lambasted the BJP leader for what he called spreading canards against Sonia. "By targeting Sonia, the BJP has indirectly admitted that they are terribly scared of her, as she will surely replace them in the immediate future," Gogoi said. "No amount of gibberish by him can influence the people of the country. Such utterances, in fact, expose the intellectual and moral bankruptcy of a party that accidentally attained power at the Centre with the help of innumerable crutches," he said.

Sonia's critics should remember that foreigners like A.O. Hume, a retired British civil servant and Annie Besant, a British theosophist were associated with the Congress. Sister Nivedita, an Irish by birth, adopted India as her home. No one raised any doubt about his or her involvement in matter of India then. The Albania-born nun Mother Teresa set up her mission in Kolkata and settled in the city considering the country as her own. After the Mother's death most Indians regard her as a saint.

Ultimately a point arises that it is not essential where you born, it is about where your emotional loyalties lie. Sonia married an Indian. So, by dint of her marriage India is her country. She gradually adapted to Indian culture. Those who made her origin an issue, forgot to understand that the ordinary people of the country were not at all bothered where she was born. For them the real issue was totally different. They are concerned about bread and butter, home, hospital, transportation, peace, progress and harmony.

Good governance is the real expectation of the people. They are sick of leaders who have reduced politics to *rath yatras*. Some people question why Sonia has been made the leader of the Congress although there is no dearth of experienced and motivated leaders. The fact is that, she belongs to the Gandhi family and it is obvious that the party will ask her to take over. The fruits of her leadership are here for all to see, peace and harmony are prevailing in the country.

When Sonia joined the Congress, the party was in complete disarray. She single-handedly brought it back to track. Today the party has been voted to power in several states. One should know that in democracy, even dynasties have to be sustained through the mechanism of ballot. People voted for the Congress preferably to be ruled by her.

Sonia may be of Italian born but she has brought up her siblings in India and after the assassination of her husband, she even refused to take them back to the land of her birth. She voluntarily surrendered her Italian passport and took Indian citizenship. By refusing to accept any post after continuous persuasion she has proved that she is not power hungry.

A large number of people had a continuous doubt about her ability and commitment to the country. That has been proved totally wrong. The most noteworthy thing is that she lives in the country and has accepted it as her domain. Sonia has been part of India's political first family for 38 years and remained with it through ups and downs. The period is long enough by any standards to become an Indian.

Commitment to the country shouldn't be one-sided. When she was in the Opposition, people didn't object to it. That she was being tipped as the future prime minister, doubts were being raised about her veracity. Why should there be any fear that she would impinge on policy matters, whether nuclear, defence or foreign affairs.

Sonia has traversed the country widely and has established good rapport with the rural masses, especially the women. She has good understanding of issues that a seasoned politician should have. By actions she has proved her affinity and loyalty to the country. She has become a popular all-India leader.

If Sonia's popularity is any indication, the people have accepted her as their leader. She is well positioned in the rural domain and criticised those for questioning her commitment to India. "I am an Indian and nobody can snatch away my Indianness from me," she declared while addressing a rally organised by women's wing of the Maharashtra Pradesh Congress Committee. She said, "Those who call themselves nationalist are afraid of a lone woman and are pointing an accusing finger at me. But I have been following Indian tradition and have fulfilled my duties as daughter-in-law of an Indian household." She further declared, "Let anybody level any accusation against me, I will remain an Indian and be true to India."

The NDA Government could have brought legislation banning foreigners from holding constitutional posts, but it didn't. To a question, then Law Minister Jana Krishnamurthi denied that the Centre had any plan to bring in any legislation on the issue.

The BJP leadership didn't want to discard Sonia's foreign origin issue just to derive political mileage out of it. That is why the party's Raipur national executive meeting in July 2003 had deliberations on her foreign origin. It even passed a resolution challenging her credential for the post of prime minister. Accordingly, the party decided to make a campaign against her claim for the post. The leaders asked party activists to convince the village people about the dangers involved in making a foreign born person as prime minister.

TRIUMPHS AND DEFEATS

After entering into active politics, Sonia has, in fact, brought miracles for the party. Several elections were fought—local, assembly and parliamentary but she scored victory in many of them. She tasted only fewer defeats. Her first and remarkable triple victory was in Delhi, Madhya Pradesh and Rajasthan in 1998. Some of the closely-contested elections are described below.

In Gujarat assembly elections in 2002, the Congress had little hopes. Even then the party gave the BJP a tough challenge. Before elections, Sonia sensibly appointed Shankersinh Vaghela as Pradesh Congress Committee (PCC) chief. Vaghela was a match for the incumbent Chief Minister Modi. Vaghela is a leader of the *Kshatriyas* who are regarded as OBCs in the state and accounts for nearly 17 per cent of the votes. Although an OBC himself, Modi didn't have a caste base. He had to rely on Hindu votes. His public rating was, however, high in comparison to Vaghela's.

Modi played the *Hindutva* card well and projected the Congress as a party that tries to placate Muslims. Vaghela, however, exploited the caste factor. In the 1988 elections when Vaghela formed the Rashtriya Janata Party, he won just four seats in the 182-member assembly. This time Vaghela campaigned as a member of the Congress party. The position, therefore, was that Modi relied on Hindu euphoria while Vaghela banked upon caste and incumbency factors. The *Hindutva* card shadowed the incumbency factors and the Congress lost the election.

The Gujarat defeat had a bearing on the Congress party. The party was little disappointed. However, it helped the high command to make a resolve to fight future elections with greater resolution. The BJP victory was not a political earthquake for the Congress party. On the basis of in-house surveys, its leadership had hoped at least to contain the saffron party, if not defeat it.

It is pertinent to mention that the Congress party made considerable inroads into the Gujarat electorate and that happened because of the foresightedness of the Congress President. She decided to contest the polls projecting Vaghela as the chief ministerial candidate to give the BJP a tough challenge. To make the contest more challenging she entered into election pacts with Pawar's NCP and Ram Vilas Paswan's Lok Janshakti Party (LJP).

The credit for the victory of the BJP was not entirely Modi's, who was widely perceived as the architect of the infamous organised massacre. Many believe that by playing the *Hindutva* card and rousing the anti-Muslim passion among the religious bigotry with the support of Sangh Parivar, the BJP made the win possible.

The Vishwa Hindu Parishad (VHP), fighting for the cause of the community, had no qualms in saying that it was its brand of *Hindutva* that did the tricks. After the successful experiment in the *Hindutva* laboratory of Gujarat, the VHP planned to make the whole country a laboratory to establish

"Hindu supremacy". Reacting to the victory, VHP leader Praveen Bhai Togadia said, "We will make laboratory of the whole country. This is our promise and our resolve." Once he said in Jaipur, "I can't waste even two days in building the laboratory. Rajasthan has already become the laboratory of the *Hindutva*."

Buoyant by the Gujarat outcome, the BJP wanted to repeat the experience in other states as well. The party first put to test the experiment in Himachal Pradesh (HP) where 98 per cent has Hindu population. Not only this, before the election the party infused new vigour in the state unit by sending party's poll strategists there. They devoted their full energy to the elections. But the results made them bite dust. The BJP tasted a shock defeat in the state. The state, which was billed as a BJP stronghold, went to the Congress kitty. The results proved that the so-called *Hindutva* wave was confined to Gujarat only.

In politically crucial Uttar Pradesh, the Congress was not in a good position but the BJP also in bad shape. It experienced shock defeat in the 2002 assembly elections where its Chief Minister Rajnath Singh made tall claims about the outcome. As the results were out, the party was relegated to the third position. The party conceded power to the Bahujan Samaj Party (BSP) with outside support. The party's defeat didn't end here. Its neighbouring Uttaranchal government also went to the Congress hand.

Another interesting development was the Kashmir election. The election was due in the state but militancy had been at its peak. The Central Government had doubt whether it would be possible to hold free and fair elections there. The election in the state virtually posed a challenge for the Centre. However, it accepted the challenge and decided to go ahead with its election plans. No political party, except the Congress could muster courage to campaign vigorously. The result was that the Congress party performed well. It became the second largest party in terms of seats won.

Besides Gujarat, the Congress party's other major defeats were Rajasthan, Madhya Pradesh and Chhattisgarh assembly elections in 2003. A notable thing to watch about is that Sonia never blames colleagues for poor show of the party. Instead she tries to send a message that it is she who should be blamed. Such magnanimity on her part can be understood from instances she has set on several occasions.

After the electoral debacle in the three states mentioned above, the CWC had a daylong session to review the reasons and to chalk out future course of action. Sonia took a practical stance, advising all the CWC members not to start blame game. She told them that the focus should be on planning out a strategy for the forthcoming General and other elections. Sonia addressed the CWC members thus:

> I have no hesitation in acknowledging that the prime responsibility for our poor performance in these elections rests with me. I am more than willing to accept whatever judgement or action the party chooses to pass or take. In owning my responsibility, I must affirm a commitment as well. Whatever position I hold or role I fulfil in the future, I will not, at any time, abandon my responsibility to our loyal workers and to the people of our country. I came into politics with a purpose—to contribute all that I could to the welfare of the people, to strengthening the party and to preserving and furthering the secular heritage and traditions of our land.
>
> My resolve in this remains unshakable. I may have made mistakes. Perhaps I could not follow my won principles outlined 18 months ago, when you first elected me Chairperson of the Congress Party in Parliament. On that occasion I pledged that our party would concentrate on working at the grass-roots level to regain the confidence of the people, to communicate our ideology and strengthen the values on which your organisation was founded. I pledge that I would rebuild our party organisation. You have honoured by once again electing me CPP leader and I will discharge this function to the best of my ability.

Elections are important in the democratic process. However, equally important and enduring are the party's goal and vision of a strong, united, secular and modern India, an India in which poverty is eradicated and all forms of exploitation—social, economic and political—are ended. Today, Congress is raising itself to meet the serious challenges facing the nation, protecting the integrity and unity of the nation, preserving its secular, pluralistic, cohesive social structures and forestalling all attempts and undermining the institutions, which have been set up to achieve these objectives.

The Congress will endeavour to evolve a broad national consensus, which is needed for sound governance of the largest pluralistic society in the world. The Congress will not allow partisan interest to come in the way of this national task. The Congress believes that all political parties dedicated to the larger national interest should work together towards ensuring the maintenance and protection of the secular and pluralistic character of society.

The Congress desires to make Indian economy strong, viable and people-oriented. Many changes are needed both in politics and programmes. Most of these issues have been identified in the 1999 election manifesto of the party. The Congress-ruled states have special responsibilities. They should not only implement their promises to the people but also set examples of good governance.

In this election our manifesto contains programmes for the benefit of farmers and industry. We will strengthen the Panchayati Raj system. It will be our endeavour that it becomes flawless. From independence till today the Congress party has used power for the development of the country and to serve the people. This has been the tradition of Nehruji, Indiraji and Rajivji. I too have pledged to follow the same path. Politics to me is a means to serve you, a struggle to uphold my principles. I am ready for it.

> The Congress vision is rooted in the idea of one nation with a unique diversity of people's creeds and cultures. Our country's strength has always been its liberal mind and its tradition of tolerance. The politics of hate is alien to our civilization.
>
> The Congress is the world's largest democratic party. Our tri-colour has flown for over a century throughout the country. The Congress party is the only guarantor of stability, unity, prosperity and social justice. Our commitment is to revive the economy and to provide basic amenities to the poorest of the poor. We believe in the empowerment of the Indian women so that they can find their rightful place as equal partners in every sphere. We particularly look to our generation of young Indians whose expectation and ambition encompass the world. We assure them of opportunity so that they can become the cutting edge of India in the new millennium.
>
> Ours is not a battle merely for votes or for public office. It is a battle for India of our dream, for the future of our children. I invite all of you to support us in this historic battle. I urge you to join hands with us so that together we may build a strong, united and resurgent India.

A fundamental assessment was made politically and organisationally. The first question asked was why the Congress went down in the battle despite the strength with which the party re-emerged as a political force between gaining power in half the states constituting the Indian Union. The think tank believed that the basic reasons for the progress was that the Congress re-asserted its ideological position, emphasising its commitment to pluralism, socialism, democracy, balanced economic reforms and a measured approach to the problems of foreign policy and security of the country. The rank and file of the party responded to this strong ideological orientation leading to the electoral victories in several states. This is the point of view the CWC reflected in its resolution.

CONCLAVES AND CONVENTIONS

Conclaves and conventions are forums where free and frank discussions take place on various issues. It is an effort to share wisdom of senior party leaders, chief ministers and cadres in order to find solutions to various problems facing the country. The exercise also helps in creating a synergy between the Centre, the State governments and the party to pursue a common goal. Whatever discussions are held in these meetings they undoubtedly get national character.

The Congress party under Sonia's leadership has held several conclaves. These conclaves provided the Congress President ideal opportunities to deliberate on different aspects of issues with the leaders and acquaint the activists with the party's perception. The conclaves were used to galvanize the activists with party's new strategy under one roof.

Sonia has utilised the conclaves to her best advantage. Through these conclaves she, in fact, tried to get feedbacks in the presence of her party colleagues so that proper plan and programme could be made for the future. These conclaves also served as a platform for her to issue directives directly to the party functionaries.

Sonia is a hard taskmaster. She constantly monitors that the Congress governments in states perform well and the chief ministers maintain their propriety. Although the party has been ruling in many states, she, however, never destabilized a single government. On the contrary, she has been largely supportive and keeping a strict vigil on their plans and programmes.

After becoming Congress chief, Sonia has so far held seven conclaves. Each one has its own significance. Whenever an important message to be given to the party functionaries or its cadres, she holds conclaves. The conclaves and conventions that have been organised are: Chief Ministers' meet, party managers' meet and block and district presidents' meet.

The first conclave was held in New Delhi in 2000. The thrust of the New Delhi conclave was on taking general review of the performance of the Congress-ruled states. Being the first conclave after Sonia became party President, great enthusiasm was seen among the leaders. The next conclave was also held in the national capital the same year. It was called to give the chief ministers directives on good governance.

In April, 2002 third conclave was held in Guwahati. The venue was chosen to signal the party's concern with the north-east states. In this conclave the party President assessed the performance of the states. The conclave kept the focus on governments' show ahead of the next round of the assembly elections in several states.

The theme of the conclave was highlighted in the Punjab, Uttaranchal, UP and Manipur assembly elections. Right through the campaign the party leadership compared the progress made by the Congress-ruled states with those ruled by the BJP. The issue gained even greater relevance since the party had 13 chief ministers that time.

The fourth conclave was held in Mt. Abu in Rajasthan in November 2002. It was here that the disinvestment of Public Sector Units (PSUs) was ruled out. Besides the BJP ruled states of Gujarat and Himachal Pradesh, the Congress governments in Madhya Pradesh, Chhattisgarh, Rajasthan and Delhi were to seek fresh mandate in 2003. Accordingly, the meeting dealt with subjects that affected the weaker sections. The socio-economic themes that impinge on rural development got prominence.

The Shimla conclave, the fifth in the line, was held in 2003. Apart from the 1998 Panchmarhi conclave, which spoke of coalition only when "absolutely necessary", this conclave deliberated on the idea of coalition arrangement. The willingness to participate in coalitions became just a declaration of intent in this conclave. Here the Congress declared that the party was ready for parliamentary election any time and called upon the like-minded parties to come together to defeat the BJP. Later this very decision proved to be an epoch-making.

Coalitions have become the rule in Indian politics and the Congress decided to accept this reality after considerable deliberation in this conclave. Earlier, the party refused to accept this inevitability. Hence the occasional assertions were given, from Panchmarhi or elsewhere, about securing a majority in the Lok Sabha and dispensing with alliances.

Sonia invited about 10,000 party representatives functioning at the block and district levels to a convention in New Delhi the same year. It was something that no Congress leader had done in the past. The entire exercise was conducted with the objective of establishing a direct rapport with the grass-root representatives in order to not only boost their morale but also to give them a feeling of involvement in the running of the party.

It was a novel method adopted by Sonia to send a clear signal to senior party functionaries working in the organisation as well as in the governments in various states that they should not ever try to undermine the party workers. In fact, she made it a point to sit through the entire duration of the session to personally acquaint herself with the viewpoint of the party functionaries.

The speakers resented before their high command the reality about some leaders who made tall claims in Delhi but did precious little back in the areas which they claim to represent. The speakers were, in fact, encouraged to put forward their viewpoints so that steps could be taken to remove their misgivings.

Several slogans with focus on the NDA Government's failures were raised in order to energize the workers who were repeatedly told that the longer the BJP ruled the country, the longer would be the misery of the people. The response of the activists got reflected in their resolve throughout the session to make Sonia the next prime minister. On her part, she minced no words.

The message that went out was "think for the country and act for the party. It is the party which makes the government and not the government that makes the party". There was another slogan: *Congress ka hath, garibon key saath*. It had shades of Indira's famous victory credo in 1971. In fact, Sonia was slowly and steadily getting into the mould of her mother-in-law who was the greatest mass leader in electoral politics in the twentieth century.

Sonia used the convention to arm the grass-root functionaries with the party's perceptions on key national and international issues. On the occasion she touched upon two crucial issues that had often created confusion among the party workers—*Hindutva* and Ayodhya. The party, she said, wanted that *status quo* be maintained on Ayodhya and would respect a judicial verdict on it. She outlined the Congress vision of secularism as a battle against communalism, fanaticism and political misuse of any religion for polarising the society.

The Congress President was judging the party's strength with every passing day. Since taking the reins of the party, Sonia had been winning back the support of Muslims, Dalits and farmers. The people of the country were now more inclined towards the party as its state governments had been showing good performance.

In the convention, Sonia identified herself completely with the functionaries and advised the ministers and party office bearers to attend functions organised at the block and district levels. She told the colleagues that they should not be stingy so far as extending courtesy to activists who actually form the backbone of the party as well as the soldiers who fight for the ideology of the Congress.

Sonia contrasted the Congress' focus on development and good governance with that of the BJP's. Her speech signalled the beginning of the Congress campaign for the next round of assembly and parliamentary elections. The session had a clear stamp of her and made categorical assertions in respect of the party's ideology as well as areas of priority, which needed to be attended to without delay. The enthusiasm and participation at the convention was vibrant.

If enthusiasm be any criterion, the mood at the conclave was much more buoyant and there were far more posters, banners and flags of the party than those of the NDA constituents, who were celebrating completion of four years in the Government. On the contrary, there was no visible sign of celebration at either the BJP's central office or at the offices of the constituents.

Now people began to recognise Sonia as a popular leader and believed that she could pose a formidable challenge to the BJP. She works hard under difficult circumstances and has become politically mature quite early than expected. She is very much in a position to lead the country through the 21st century—as visualized by her husband. Not satisfied with the Vajpayee-led NDA Government, more and more people wanted Sonia to lead the nation. The party's veteran leaders were solidly behind her and that was a strength for her.

Annoyed and anguished with the directionless politics of the BJP and knowing that it was only Congress that had traditionally cared for their rights, many leaders joined the party. To name a few, one of the most popular Muslim leaders from UP, Akbar Ahmed Dumpy, joined the Congress with his large followers. Dalit leader from Delhi, Jaikishan, also came into the Congress fold.

The sixth conclave was held in Chandigarh in October 2005 after the Congress-led UPA Government remained in office for over one year. All the chief ministers of the Congress-ruled states participated in the conclave. Sonia called this conclave to take stock of the implementation level of the party's manifesto in these states. She also reviewed the performance report to the chief ministers. She wants that those have been given responsibility of a task they must execute it with sincerity and honesty. She has strong aversion for violation of the rule of law or basic tenets of the propriety.

The conclave was meant to brief the chief ministers on how to go about implementing programmes for the *aam admi* so that they don't let down the government in the next elections. The leadership was concerned at any possible erosion in its mass base. A review of the implementation of the party's programmes for the socially disadvantaged sections was already overdue. So the conclave served twin purpose—one, to activate the set-up to clear all remaining programmes and second, to put the organisation for the next election mode. The conclave also discussed crucial issues that were affecting the people like starvation death in Andhra Pradesh and power problem in Delhi.

On conclusion, Sonia described the conclave very purposeful as it served to find out the status of implementation of the manifesto, which the party promised to the people. That was precisely the object of holding the conclave.

The Nainital conclave of the Chief Ministers of Congress-ruled states held in September 2006 was seventh in the line. Besides 14 Chief Ministers, the Prime Minister, several Union Ministers and AICC leaders in charge of states attended the meeting. The two-day meeting discussed wide-ranging issues including internal security, relations with Pakistan, farmers' problem and economic development. In the conclave the main focus was rural India for which Sonia has high priority. Agriculture and internal security were the issues discussed quite prominently. The leaders also discussed strategy to be adopted in the coming assembly polls in at least four states.

According to Sonia, the UPA Government had already taken several initiatives in the farm sector and the positive impact on the growth of agriculture would be noticed soon. She was very much concerned about the low production of food grain, as a result the Centre had to import wheat. She wants to address problems of the farm sector on a priority basis so that growing food security can be ensured, as the population of the country will reach 1.4 billion after 20 years. She finds that the institutional credit for small and marginal farmers are very low as a result the crop insurance coverage is just 10 per cent of the farmers. The National Commission of Farmers (NCF) headed by eminent agricultural scientist M.S. Swaminathan has submitted four reports, which awaits serious consideration and it is likely that the Government will come out with a new agricultural policy. The NCF suggestion include setting up of farmers' commission in each state and fixing of credit with annual rate at 4 per cent besides insurance scheme for all crops and determination of minimum support price so that farmers' regular income can be protected. She urged that focus should be laid on agriculture in the 11th Five Year Plan and also called upon the chief ministers to unleash a second green revolution in their states and also emphasised on the need to strengthen the Public Distribution System (PDS).

On Special Economic Zone (SEZ) her view was that though the industry required land for expansion such moves shouldn't jeopardize farm prospects. Issuing a cautious note she said that for developing SEZs, the governments should take extra care in acquiring farmers' prime land and also urged the chief ministers to ensure that farmers get proper compensation for their land. She further added that farmers could be given stakes in projects set up on land acquired from them. She also felt the need for complete overhaul of land administration. About suicides by farmers in some states she said it was a challenge to the collective conscience and called for immediate action.

On dialogue with Pakistan, Sonia said it was desirable but care had to be taken that it didn't compromise on country's security. She supported Prime Minister's move to resume talks with Pakistan President but at the same time concerned about terrorist attacks in different parts of the country by Pakistan-based outfits.

On minority bashing, Sonia said that no community should feel being under siege because of the terrorism. She, however, cautioned that while pursuing terrorists, care had to be taken so that no innocent persons of a particular community were harassed or implicated. She was of the view that there should be no compromise on internal security and stressed upon creating motivated forces to combat terrorism.

JAN SAMPARK ABHIYAN

Sonia coined a mass contact programme to have greater reach. She drew up the strategy based on the declaration she made at the Shimla conclave that the Congress was ready to face elections any time. Keeping this assertion in mind she conceived the programme and called it *Jan Sampark Abhiyan*. Under this programme she visited remote areas and had interaction with the people of different strata to make her aware of their problems. Quite a wide area was covered at a time and people came in large numbers to see her, to hear her and to apprise her of their difficulties.

Through the *Abhiyan*, Sonia herself became known to a vast section of the population across the country. The emotion with which she spoke of her mother-in-law and husband evoked a tremendous response, especially among the women. By her emotionally surcharged addresses she could easily win the confidence of the people. It gave a big advantage to her. Seeing the overwhelming response, she realised that if the goodwill were transferred into votes, her party would certainly make some impact in the elections.

Sonia was expecting General elections in the second half of 2004, so she started the *Abhiyan* in January itself. Seeing the Congress morale down after the defeat in the three states, namely Rajasthan, M.P. and Chhattisgarh, the BJP top brass wanted to use the opportunity to their advantage. When it finally decided to call the elections early Sonia converted the *Abhiyan* into an election campaign.

Election Show-down

5

GENERAL ELECTIONS

India is a democratic country. In a democracy, the sovereignty rests with the people. It is they who accept or reject a ruler. In a democratic set-up people's representatives are elected through the process of election. In India General Elections create great enthusiasm among the people throughout the country. Statutory agency, the Election Commission (EC), conducts the election. Through franchise the country's voters pick up lawmakers of their choice for next five years.

The 14th General Elections created a sensation in the history of Indian democracy. Throughout the elections and afterwards many interesting developments took place, which should remain written in the pages of history. Besides these, various aspects of Sonia's leadership ability were reflected ushering in the new era of value-based politics that she fervently believes in. Some relevant process of the elections is described here.

Free and fair elections are reflective of vibrant democracy. So it should be held in such an atmosphere that people can coolly evaluate parties and candidates for their respective agenda and programmes and the contestants too can canvass for support on a secular basis and within the constraints defined by the EC as well as under the well-established political norms.

The EC announced schedule for the General Elections at the end of February 2004. After the announcement, the code of conduct came into effect. Without wasting time, all the political parties were on their toes for making alliances, selecting winnable candidates and shaping up attractive slogans to woo the voters over the next 45 odd days.

Salient features of the elections are given: Seats—543, electorate—67.15 crore, contesting candidates—5,435, polling stations—6,87,402, counting centres—1,214, EVMs used—10.75 lakh, expenditure—1,300 crore.

There are many political parties in the country but the contest is thrilling between the big two—the BJP and the Congress. Both the parties had formed their alliances. The BJP-led NDA was a ruling party. Its alliance partners comprised more than 20 parties. The BJP alone aimed to win around 300 seats.

The Congress party effected some changes in the campaign programme. The party gave more stress on projecting image of Sonia. Last time it was just rallies but for this election she went for mass contact through the *Jan Sampark Abhiyan.*

Under the *Abhiyan* Sonia began travelling various parts of the country. Wherever she went, tremendous response was noticed among the people. The ordinary people would wait on the roadside in large numbers and intermittently stopped her to tell their problems. The womenfolk showed particular interest in her.

On the other hand Sonia had to face adverse publicity campaign during this time. The BJP leaders were exaggerating the claims of their achievements. To give the Congress a tough challenge, the NDA Government launched huge budgeted advertisement campaign. Its 'India Shining' and 'Bharat Udai' campaigns were given maximum publicity. Advani went for a high-tech Rath Yatra and caught wide media attention.

Sonia had to endure their vitriolic remarks and insinuations for her Italian origin. Her opponents launched sinister campaign about her ability and propriety to run the country. They left no stone unturned to portray her in negative angles.

To counter it Sonia began rather a systematic and sober publicity. In her election meetings, she stressed mainly on common people's problems like unemployment, farmers' difficulties, backwardness and social harmony. The slogans *Congress ke hath, garibon ke saath* and *Aam admi ko kya mila* were well received by the masses.

Sonia was able to influence the choice of a large number of women, especially in the rural areas. She secured almost automatic support of overwhelming sections of Muslims and Christians because of the memories of the Gujarat pogrom were not wiped out by the presence of a few second and third ranked Muslim leaders in the BJP.

With the *Abhiyan*, Sonia ensured constant familiarity with average Indians. It is this group that has the sufficient strength to tilt the balance in which side they go. The plank Sonia chose was the one where she negated the whole concept of NDA Government's 'Feel Good' by asking people to introspect if they were really feeling good and if their India was really shining. It was this connection that she persuaded with greater vigour.

Sonia's political maturity was evident for several years as some of her decisions proved right and beneficial. The Congress pact with the People's Democratic Party (PDP) to form a coalition government in J & K and with the NCP in Maharashtra to form a government there showed it all. These decisions were the outcome of extensive consultations she had with colleagues and wider set of people.

Sonia's decision to go for a coalition pact in J & K was a shining example of her maturity. The country's polity is such that coalition politics has become a compulsion. She knew it very well that without a solid coalition the Congress couldn't hope of returning to power. That is why she entered into coalition pact before the General elections and even at later stages she never hesitated to enter into electoral understandings.

Sonia took many bold decisions and those struck well. Her decisions helped to portray her as a successful leader. This image was enough to counter the mighty image of Vajpayee. The BJP's poor record in the governance was another factor that made many people veer towards the Congress. Outside the urban middle-class, the question of her origin had become something of a non-issue.

It was discernable from the very beginning that Sonia had multi-faceted versatility. Being a political novice, it was quite unthinkable for anyone that Sonia would surpass Vajpayee in popularity. Vajpayee is an asset for his party, so is she for hers. But when a comparison is drawn between the two, she didn't lag behind. She established informal and close contacts with the populace more quickly than imagined.

Sonia became synonymous with the developmental work. Among the achievements that could be counted were education, road construction, power generation and most of all drought management. In a democratic country it is achievement that matters and not birth. People of many states have seen how the developmental work took place during the Congress government's tenure.

The mood among the BJP leadership was high because their alliance had successfully run the coalition government. The party considered it a great achievement as no other coalition governments could run for so long. The other achievements they talked about were: Pokhran nuclear test, defeat of Pakistan in Kargil, isolation of Pakistan in the international fora, mobilisation of world opinion in favour of a permanent United Nations Security Council seat, successful holding of assembly elections in J & K, enactment of the Prevention of Terrorism Act (POTA), five per cent annual economic growth in spite of earthquakes, floods and droughts etc. and the successful sending of satellites into orbit.

The Congress, however, considered that the BJP-led NDA Government had come a cropper in implementing the promises made to the people. The BJP, however, maintained that the Government had drawn up a series of ambitious infrastructure development programmes like the Golden Quadrilateral Project and the Prime Minister's Grameen Rojgar Yojana (PMGRY) etc. All such projects had generated considerable employment opportunities. The BJP argued that it would take some time to quantify the opportunities, adding that there was no reason to be despondent on the employment generation front. It is worth mentioning that Prime Minister, during his Independence Day address from the ramparts of the Red Fort in 2001, had announced that his Government would strive to create one crore jobs every year.

The BJP came to power by promising clean government, building of Ram temple at Ayodhya, end of militancy once and for all and creation of job opportunities every year, but what the people understood after five years of rule was that it had failed on all fronts. On the domestic front, the Government had not put down militancy. The Pokhran nuclear test was received by Pakistan as a challenge. It responded by conducting as many as five nuclear tests to even the account with India.

The Congress and other Opposition parties began to accuse the Vajpayee Government of taking India to the brink of nuclear confrontation. Because of this the Government decided to tackle the situation diplomatically. It called back its High Commissioner to Pakistan, asked Pakistan to reduce the strength of its diplomatic staff in New Delhi to half and banned Pakistan Airlines to use Indian airspace. Pakistan, in turn, imposed similar restrictions for India.

Scams like coffin scam, petrol pump scam and land scam were enough to substantiate people's disillusion about the NDA Government. The Tehelka.com expose involving the then BJP President Bangaru Lakshman and others was another glaring example of the Government's wrongdoings. The Congress-led Opposition parties demanded sacking of then Defence Minister for his role in influencing defence deals. Although Fernandes resigned, Vajpayee reinstated him after a few months.

Advani who spearheaded the Ram temple movement in 1990, assured people that if the party came to power it would find an amicable solution to the vexed Ram Janmabhoomi issue and build a grand temple. The BJP was in power and Advani being the second most powerful person in the Government, failed to find an amicable solution to it.

For a good show, the Congress wanted a partner in UP, while the BJP decided to go solo. The Congress wanted an understanding with either the SP or the BSP but it could not be reached.

Straight fights and multi-cornered contests apart, for 293 seats either the BJP or the Congress struck alliances. The Congress was now willing to switch over to coalition politics after its defeat in the three states. It cobbled together allies for as many as 210 seats spread across east, west, north and south India: Andhra Pradesh, Bihar, Jammu and Kashmir, Jharkhand, Kerala, Maharashtra and Tamil Nadu.

The BJP was better placed—it had allies in 253 seats expanding over Andhra Pradesh, Bihar, Maharashtra, Orissa, West Bengal, Punjab, Tamil Nadu and the north-east. In many states, the BJP was either non-existent or a minor partner to a strong regional ally—in states like Kerala, Tamil Nadu, Orissa, Punjab, West Bengal and the North-East which account for total 188 seats.

BJP VS CONGRESS

The growth of the BJP in the 1990s had been phenomenal as it emerged at the centre stage of politics and created ground for a bipolar policy in the country. Earlier an era of single dominant party under the Congress regime was prevailing.

Both Vajpayee and Advani are the assets of the BJP while Sonia is alone considered the same for the Congress. Ideologically both the parties are far apart. The BJP calls the Congress pseudo-secular while the Congress calls the BJP communal. The BJP had the experience of running a coalition government and the Congress went to elections heading an alliance for the first time. The battle line was drawn even before the election dates were announced. Who stood where was pretty clear. The picture that emerged was of a distinctly multi-polar polity, dependent on coalition politics. Technically either of them would lead the next government.

Vajpayee and Advani were politically more experienced than Sonia. Vajpayee is in politics from his school days and

Advani's political experience spans five decades. On the other hand Sonia entered into politics after crossing 50. Although she belongs to the premier political family she maintained a distance from it for as long as 30 years.

It was for the fourth time in succession that the BJP had been seeking votes under Vajpayee. The first time was in 1996 when the party emerged as the single largest party. Vajpayee became Prime Minister but couldn't garner majority in the stipulated time, so the Government lasted only for 13 days. The second time was in 1998 when the party managed to get majority but lasted only for 13 months. Third time was in 1999 when the BJP came to power heading a coalition that is NDA. Vajpayee Government lasted curtailed term. He remained the most preferred leader throughout the country.

Terming the last mandate secured by the NDA as the 'trailer', Advani said the present elections were the 'real test' for the NDA, as it was seeking support on the basis of its performance and good governance. The BJP was taking pride that it remained the 'longest serving non-Congress government' and 'first-ever alliance government to survive so many years'. The party's claim was that it had successfully run the alliance government with partners having different ideologies.

The Congress, however, criticised the BJP saying that Vajpayee never remained consistent. Several times Sonia alleged that he changed stand very often. What he said one day, within a few days he back tracked from his statement. Some of his utterances are produced here.

Vajpayee told a Sangh Parivar gathering in New York on September 9, 2000: "My right to remain Swayam Sevak cannot be taken away." This was explained away later to mean that he was a Swayam Sevak of the country.

On August 26, 2001 Vajpayee said in Lucknow apropos of Fernandes: There is no question of his return to the Government till...all allegations against him are cleared." He also said: "Talks are going on at various levels to find a solution on Ayodhya issue before March 2002." Fernandes was reinducted shortly. On his later statement both the Muslim Personal Law Board and the VHP denied Vajpayee's claim the very next day.

Muslims were warned on February 19, 2002 that the BJP could win the UP assembly elections without their support, but would like to secure it. Vajpayee made that statement as Prime Minister was really unfortunate. His party, however, lost the mandate in the elections that followed. Though a ruling party in the state, it was relegated to the third position and conceded power to the BSP's Mayawati with outside support.

At close looking it was found that the two parties directly faced each other only in six north Indian states that accounted for a mere 102 seats out of a total of 543. Six more constituencies in Arunachal Pradesh and Union Territories had a head-on contest between the big two parties.

The Congress party had an alliance with Dravida Munnetra Kazhagam (DMK) in Tamil Nadu and Pondicherry. The party already had a coalition pact in Kerala. In Karnataka the battle was mainly between the Congress and H.D. Deve Gowda's Janata Dal (Secular). These states together have 130 seats. In 1999 the Congress went alone to the elections and got only 33 seats. With the election tie-ups this time round, the party was upbeat about its electoral prospects in the south.

In Maharashtra the Congress had seat-sharing pact with the NCP. In 1999 the party contested the elections alone and got only 15 seats out of 48. The Congress-NCP government was going well in the state and unanimity prevailed among the leaders of both the parties, so good performance was expected from the alliance.

The BJP didn't like the Congress' decision to have alliances with other political parties. When the Congress had tie-up with the Telengana Rashtra Samiti (TRS), the BJP made all sorts of derision, saying the Congress was trying to ride piggyback on regional outfits and that it was unable to prevent the exit of its leaders to other parties.

The BJP was so sure of its success that it began to advise the Congress to introspect as to why its leaders were leaving the party, indirectly referring to the then Rajya Sabha Deputy Chairperson Najma Heptullah who then joined the BJP. The then BJP Spokesman Arun Jaitley said, "The Congress has to analyse why people are leaving the party or why those stepping into politics are not getting attracted to it."

However, the situation wasn't rosy for both the BJP and the Congress in the Hindi belt. Historically, Uttar Pradesh with 80 or 15 per cent of the total Lok Sabha seats always plays a key role in the government formation. The state's political landscape was fragmented: In the 2002 assembly elections, the Samajwadi Party topped the list without a majority of its own, followed by the Bahujan Samajwadi Party (BSP), the BJP and the Congress came in that order. The Congress had no tie-up with any party in the state. In case of any pact, it might have had an advantage over the BJP.

The Congress was a bit demoralised after its defeat in the three states. All these states account for 65 Lok Sabha seats. The Congress won 21 seats in the 1999 elections.

As the NDA was a ruling party, its leaders remained focused on the print as well as on the electronic media. Both Vajpayee and Advani were star campaigners. They enjoyed high stature in the country's politics. For his knack in development, Vajpayee began to be known as *Vikash Purush* and for unflinching authority Advani was called *Lauh Purush* in the political circle. The BJP's second-rung leaders were well-experienced and able poll strategists.

Sonia was the only star campaigner for her party. The odds with her were: She is not of Indian origin, politically inexperienced in comparison to Vajpayee and Advani, and did not get wider media coverage. Congress' second-rung leaders were well experienced and able to give the rivals tough challenge.

Logistically the BJP campaigners were more systematic and mobile. The Congress had no access to enough transport facilities. The BJP exaggerated claims of achievements of its

Government. The party, through its advertisement campaign, transcended the voters' capacity to perceive ground realities and came to their own judgement. Sonia's response to the blitzkrieg, which was backed by advertisement and campaign budget of over Rs. 250 crore, remained systematic and sober rather than high-flying and glamorous. The BJP not only perniciously emphasised Sonia's foreign origin, but blown it out of proportion, accompanied by personal attacks on her and her children.

Money plays a big role in elections and the BJP used it for its own benefit. The NDA Government spent lavishly on advertisements through ministries highlighting its achievements. The advertisements appeared in newspapers and TV channels well in advance, before the election schedule was announced. The Congress party moved the EC with the allegation that the advertisements were a burden on the exchequer. The EC, however, objected to it citing violation of norms for free and fair elections. When Vajpayee's attention was drawn towards it, he justified it saying: "It is part of the Government's duty that it should put its achievements before the people."

ELECTION STRATEGY

At the end of December 2003, Sonia started consulting colleagues regarding the election strategy. She constituted a manifesto committee, a campaign committee and organised a cell in the AICC to draw up a detailed all-India campaign programme well in advance. She entrusted these tasks to the leaders on the basis of previous performance.

Congress poll managers: Sonia remained involved in the campaign. She had set up several panels and informal groups to monitor campaign. Still hers was the first and last word.

Ambika Soni ran Sonia's office and media department, which was the key to party's election management.

Ahmed Patel, Sonia's political secretary, was part of every strategy and monitoring group. Party matters were routed through him.

Manmohan Singh's stature as a renowned economist came handy. He was crucial for making the Congress vision document.

Arjun Singh was on key AICC committees set up for elections. He was one of the key members brokering alliances.

Salman Khurshid prepared, vetted or used inputs any document that went into Sonia's hand.

Pranab Mukherjee, the man for all seasons. He was involved in resolving all issues and problems.

S. Jaipal Reddy, a rich experienced and witty politician, was always ready for whatever job entrusted with.

Jairam Ramesh was involved in publicity campaigns. The Hindi inputs for speeches came from Janardhan Dwivedi.

The BJP was not election ready because of its high command remained undecided for quite a long time whether the election time be advanced or not. When they finally decided on early elections, the leaders started thinking seriously for plans and programmes. Moreover, the leaders took Sonia lightly and were sure that their party or the NDA would stage a comeback.

Both the BJP and the Congress leaders were now ready for the face off. The mood was optimistic in the BJP camp. The party was banking upon Vajpayee's charisma and his ability to run coalition government. The party leadership believed that Sonia was an immature politician and had no grass-roots apprenticeship, which every politician enjoys as a matter of course and also she lacked political judgement, both by instinct as well as by training. All successful leaders have an intrinsic political judgement but Sonia had none. In mass politics, political sense is important. It gives one a feel for timing, ability to take risk and to discern popular undercurrents. Sonia didn't seem to have it. BJP leaders felt that strong sense of privacy was Sonia's biggest handicap.

The BJP has weakness too. It doesn't have all-India presence as the Congress has. At the time of elections the Congress was ruling in 14 states and the BJP only in six. In south and north-east, the BJP had little presence. The Congress was better off in these areas. In UP, Bihar and West Bengal, both the parties' state units were weak. Lok Sabha seats from these states make up 162 out of a total 543. If the five seats of Uttaranchal and 14 seats of Jharkhand are added the number becomes 181—34 per cent of the total seats. In these states, except West Bengal, the BJP has larger presence compared to the Congress.

In West Bengal, Chief Minister Buddhadeb Bhattacharjee proved to be a good administrator. The CPI (M) has been ruling the state at a stretch for over 27 years. Trinamool Congress supremo Mamta Banerjee's popularity was on the decline and people began to consider her as unreliable.

In Bihar, Lalu Prasad Yadav's Rashtriya Janata Dal (RJD) was well placed. The party was ruling the state for second term. The RJD is a regional party and had an alliance with the Congress. It was being expected that the alliance would show good performance.

In Punjab the Congress government was doing well. Its rival, the Akali Dal, was out of power for two years and its hold in the state had declined considerably. Under such a situation the Congress party's prospect seemed to be brighter there.

The same situation prevailed in Uttaranchal where Congress' N.D. Tiwari was considered a seasoned politician. Quite a good show was being expected from the state.

In Orissa, Naveen Patnaik of the Biju Janata Dal (BJD) was facing an uphill task in creating a wave in favour of his party.

In Assam, veteran Congress leader Tarun Gogoi was doing well. During his rule, the economy had made a significant progress despite the state faced major problems like terrorism, unemployment and influx of refugees.

The same was the case with Ajit Jogi, the former Congress Chief Minister of Chhattisgarh. He was banking upon good job he did, like setting up of large industrial base.

In Delhi, Sheila Dikshit's performance was satisfying. The Congress was expecting to do well as her government made lot of progress in the field of infrastructure development, transport and pollution control, besides solving power and water problem. By privatising the power distribution system, the situation in the power sector improved considerably.

In Haryana, the Indian National Lok Dal (INLD) government headed by Om Prakash Chautala feared anti-incumbency wave. Senior leader Bhajan Lal of the Congress was appointed the PCC chief. He was set to give Chautala a tough fight.

In Himachal Pradesh, the Congress' Vir Bhadra Singh was heading the government. In the 2002 assembly elections, the Congress gave the BJP a humiliating defeat. The party was sure to make some impact.

Andhra Pradesh was for a tough fight between the Telugu Desam Party (TDP) and the Congress. State Chief Minister Chandrababu Naidu feared anti-incumbency wave.

In Tamil Nadu there was always a sea-saw battle between Jayalalitha and M. Karunanidhi. Jayalalitha had the upper hand but the Congress-DMK pact posed a challenge to her.

In Gujarat, the BJP had 20 out of the 26 Lok Sabha seats. The party was quite comfortable about the election outcome because of its smooth victory in the last assembly elections.

In Madhya Pradesh, the BJP had 21 seats out of 29. The *bijli-pani-sadak* facility holds the key to the outcome of the election results.

In Rajasthan, the party had 16 out of 25 seats. The BJP was in doubt if it would be able to retain so many seats again.

In smaller states like Meghalaya, Tripura and Mizoram, the BJP had little presence as compared to the Congress.

ELECTION FEVER

After selection of candidates and filing of nomination papers were over, the party leaders and the candidates began vigorous campaigning. Besides big rallies and corner meetings, the candidates took advantage of the IT industry in making direct contact with the electorate.

Soon the election fever gripped the nation. The Congress came out with songs. One is here: *Ye jo public hai sab janti hai, BJP kya hai, Tehelka kya hai, Judeo kya hai, tauba karo sab janti hai*. According to Congress' Khurshid, the party had two-pronged strategy. In the first phase, there were nine posters plus slogans highlighting unemployment, plight of farmers and insecurity of women. Besides, there were SMSs, CDs and cassettes based on popular songs. In the second phase, the party showcased the positive aspects of the Congress regime.

Congress election CDs had images of Rajiv making an appeal for Sonia with the tune of *Kar chale hum fida jaan aur tan saathiyon.... Nazar aaunga mein Sonia vesh mein, Yeh karegi tumhara har swapna pura*...and parody spoofed from Nana Patekar's famous lines in the film *Yashwant: Ek machchar ne aadmi ko....*

Remixes of popular filmy songs were made to catch public attention. Both the BJP and the Congress used them extensively. The BJP remix was made thus: *Dilli ke angan mein Congress ka kya kaam hai; bijli-paani mein to Congress badnam hai.*

The Congress had this: *Dilli ke rajniti mein BJP ka kya kaam hai, yeh to ghapla, ghotala aur tabut mein badnam hai.*

The BJP targeted Sonia's origin with *Tum to thahre pardesi, Sarkar kya chalaogi?*

Congress responded thus: *Tum to thahre Vajpayee, tum toh bhag jaoge; wada jo karte ho woh nahi nibhaoge.*

Even party symbols were not spared. Taking on BJP's symbol, the Congress came out with *Le jayenge, le jayenge, tera phool udakar le jayenge; Reh jayenge, reh jayenge, Vajpayeeji dekhte reh jayenge. Tum ho kali to nabab hum hai, phoolon ko masal dale woh haath hum hai.*

Some more Congress numbers: *Bachke rehna re baba bachke rehna re, NDA ki chaal se ab bachke rehna re* and *Japte Ram ka naam, karte ulta kaam.*

The BJP had another one: *Bari bari, Atal Behari*. In the 90s the BJP urged the voters saying *Abki bari, Atal Behari.*

Other parties also developed innovative tricks to get maximum attention. Local and national issues got least prominence in the campaigns.

Film and television actors were in great demands. The BJP candidates banked upon the 'star' campaigners to get them votes. Film actress and Rajya Sabha member Hema Malini was the first choice followed by actors Shatrughan Sinha and Vinod Khanna.

The BJP was successful in its attempt to woo the Muslim voters by inducting some of the community's leaders to its fold. The basic purpose behind this was to influence public opinion that it was not a communal party but a secular one and the party succeeded to some extent in its attempt.

ELECTION MANIFESTO

Election manifesto is a white paper of promises prepared by the parties. The manifesto provides the electorate a clear idea about what the party will do if voted to power. Every political party prepares manifesto with great care so that it reflects its policies and programmes in clear perspective, at the same time catches the imagination of the electorate.

The BJP brought out its manifesto as a 'Vision Document'. A Committee of second rung leaders prepared the document. It looked like Vajpayee's photo album. The document featured as many as 55 photographs of the *Vikas Purush*. However, the 'glorification' didn't please him. In fact it annoyed him. To clear the embarrassment, the party released a new document a week later with just two photographs of Vajpayee.

The BJP gave much weight to the NDA agenda. It was about good governance, development and peace. Vajpayee released it a few days later after the release of Vision Document. The NDA agenda reflected the party's dominance. It also included the Ayodhya issue. He publicly defended the move saying building of Ram temple was a public and national issue. NDA Convenor George Fernandes defended it saying no one could object to the stand on it, as it would strengthen national integration.

On the other hand, Sonia was aware of the difficulties being faced by the *aam admi* (common people). She got this insight during her *Jan Sampark Abhiyan*. She came to understand that a greater chunk of the people remained out of work and so live a penury life. She felt that something should be done for their uplift, without which real progress of the country was not possible. When the party prepared the manifesto, she took utmost care that pro-poor schemes were incorporated in it.

Sonia released the Congress manifesto on March 22. It was a package of promises, old and new, to be fulfilled within an issue-specific time frame. The party promised for creating jobs, repairing the country's fiscal health and devising an action plan for governance.

Assuring one crore jobs every year, the 32-page document remained unwavering in its focus on employment generation and infusing new life into the farm sector—issues on which the party had repeatedly rapped the BJP. In a major pitch to rural voters, who remained untouched by the NDA's 'Feel good' claim, the Congress promised employment for 100 days every year to every rural household at a minimum wage.

The driving objective behind the document—to be followed by issue specific vision statements—was to raise questions over the BJP's 'India Shining' and 'Feel Good' slogans. Towards that end, it contrasted the achievements under Congress regimes with that of the NDA's 'monumental' failures on the social, economic, political, institutional and foreign policy fronts. Novel features included promises for progress reports on every May Day (on employment) and Gandhi Jayanti (on the manifesto as a whole).

On Ayodhya, the Congress reaffirmed its faith in the judicial process, stating that out of court negotiations should be between the parties to the dispute. Sonia wanted that such talks should have the force of law.

The other promises were reservation in private sector for Dalits and tribals, steps for easing debt burden, reservation of one-thirds parliamentary and assembly seats for women, more transparent foreign direct investment (FDI), 8-10 per cent

GDP growth rate each year and hike in outlay on education up to six per cent of the GDP etc.

ELECTIONEERING

Electioneering is the most crucial stage of the election process. It literally takes the candidates to doorsteps of the electorate. While the big leaders confine themselves to big rallies, the second line leaders and the regional satraps try to bridge the gap with the electorate in projecting their USP (unique selling proposition) and highlighting the rivals' flipsides.

The BJP left no stone unturned to point out Sonia's deficiencies. Arun Jaitley was emphatic that her foreign birth might seriously impinge on whatever decisions she would take, whether economic, defence, nuclear or foreign affair. "It is a matter of national security if she becomes prime minister," he said.

Jaitley always saw red about Sonia's ability to lead the country and jeered at her for making speeches from prepared text and for constant tutoring. He once said, "You cannot have as prime minister a person about whose comprehension and understanding there is a definite doubt."

The Congress election managers focussed all their energies on *Jan Sampark Abhiyan*. It was noticed that for the first time Sonia, the highly protected public leader, tried to break through the security cordon and reach out to people. The cadres and general public responded with great enthusiasm. The *Abhiyan* literally overshadowed the 'India Shining' campaign launched by the BJP.

Sonia has excellent rapport with the cadres and has instinctive feel for politics. She has put in place a unique mechanism for getting feedback that is same as mass contact. She chairs most meetings with the cadres and take feedback from them.

The Congress media managers concentrated heavily on the regional media. Beginning with the *aam admi ko kya mila* campaign which highlighted the BJP-NDA's colossal failure, they harked back to the past, began with *Congress ke raj mein hui hamari sunvayi* and ended with the catchy one line *Mein Congress ke saath hoon*. Youth, women, farmers and the middle-classes were the focus of the campaign, though not necessarily in that order.

Vajpayee, the BJP patriarch, played the stability card. He said in numerous election rallies, "Leaders of non-NDA parties are more interested in grabbing power than governance. All political parties and their leaders are busy presenting themselves as prospective aspirants for the post of prime minister. Now it is time for you to judge who is really capable of providing a stable government. The last five years have proved that the BJP is not a bogey for minorities." He also said that the Opposition parties were raking up the Gujarat issue in order to confuse the minorities.

During electioneering, the opposition critics stooped to the extent of maligning Sonia and the family she married into. Some BJP leaders resorted to 'low level' personalized campaign. Unleashing vitriolic attack Narendera Modi called Sonia daughter of Italy. On this the Congress accused him saying that he had lost his sense of proportion and mental balance. He, however, justified his outburst, saying it was a political statement made in the heat of an election campaign and not a personal observation. He relented saying, "There was nothing personal about my observations, I only spoke out against the Congress President. Is she not the Congress President? Is she not the daughter of Italy? There was nothing wrong in what I said." He said that his intention was to take head-on in the political battle.

The Congress launched scathing attack on opponent parties by charging them with showing 'utter disregard' for the Constitution, the Supreme Court judgement and the people's will in deciding who would be the prime minister. The Congress said by raking up Sonia's foreign issue, these parties had violated all norms.

The Congress criticised the BJP for questioning the Indianness of the leader of the country's oldest and largest political party and Leader of the Opposition. Unlike her detractors, Sonia had won elections with thumping margins after entering into politics. "She doesn't require a certificate of Indianness from people who are in politics with pernicious agenda of holding the country to ransom. Past poll results have shown the acceptability of her as leader in the country," the party charged.

No matter who says what, Sonia remains indifferent to such criticisms and never retorts back. However she welcomes constructive criticism because it helps in drawing policies. When addresses political meetings, she never accuse anyone personally. She always acts according to principle and conviction. Only subjects concerning the *aam admi* are her talking points. She never dithers to condemn the opponents when she finds something deficient or misuse of authority on their part. Even when she criticises, she does so in a dignified and restrained manner. These are the qualities which distinguish her from the rest.

"Instead of development, the BJP-led NDA Government had shut down industries, increased unemployment, raised prices and spread the poison of communalism in society," Sonia charged at a rally and immediately made rapport with her audience.

"If the Congress comes to power, it would fulfil all its promises, including creating communal harmony, providing employment to the youth, uplifting the weaker sections, empowering women and ensuring economic development," she said at another rally amidst chorus of *Sonia Gandhi Zindabad*.

Sonia asked voters to grill BJP leaders when they visit them to seek votes. "Ask them (BJP leaders) what they have done for the development of the country and the states and how much the *aam admi* has benefited under them," she urged the electorate.

"Even the farmers were deprived of proper price for their produce. The poor, the minority and the women have not benefited under the NDA," she lamented. Focusing on the achievements of her party, she said though the Congress had faced many ups and downs, it never wavered from its ideology and commitment to the people.

Striking the sentimental chord in Chennai, Sonia said she would feel honoured if she met the same fate that had befallen her husband at nearby Seriperimbudur. "I feel it an honour to stand on this soil in which the blood of my husband had mingled. There could be no greater honours if I meet with the same fate. The life and dreams of Rajivji were the source of great inspiration to me. I carry forward the dreams he had in mind for India," she said. She also said, "Those who abuse me and the family to which I belong, I will say that I feel honoured in belonging to that family which had lived and died for the country."

The election was basically a contest between the Congress and the BJP and for that matter between Sonia and Vajpayee. A variety of issues were raised to mould the mind of the electorate. Sonia was not at all perturbed with the sinister campaign perpetrated by her detractors and said that she would continue to be in politics and serve the people despite the NDA's criticism. *Mujhe in logon ka koi dar nahin hai* (I am not afraid of these people), she declared. "I have not entered into politics for power but to continue the family tradition of serving the poor and the downtrodden," she said.

Sonia said that the NDA was 'trying its best' to divert the people's attention from the people's real problems. "What the BJP and its allies are doing at present is to blame Congress for everything," she said. In reference to the attacks on the minorities, she expressed concern saying, "Communal and divisive forces have become active." She called upon the people to remain watchful so that such forces wouldn't gain strength. Saying that poverty and unemployment were the two major problems facing the people, she claimed the situation would improve if the Congress were voted to power.

Addressing a rally Sonia said the Congress was in need of the people's support to lead the nation into a "future of prosperity and happiness". Stating that the party was aware of the basic needs of different neglected sections like weavers, fishermen, rural artisans and farmers, she said it had formulated policies for their uplift and incorporated them in its manifesto. She said her party would give a thrust to the concept of Panchayati Raj if voted to power. She reminded the people that it was Rajiv who had canalised the flow of funds directly to Village Panchayats for implementation and development work.

Touching upon the Congress manifesto, she said that the party was committed to providing free education to the deprived sections, from the primary to university level. She said that the Congress had always stood by the Scheduled Castes, Scheduled Tribes and other backward castes and would pursue the same policy. She asserted that women would be given their due representation in legislative bodies and declared that the party itself had provided substantial number of seats for women in the present elections.

The BJP leadership began to see it politically unwise to antagonise nearly 12 per cent of the Muslim population who in some areas, including politically crucial UP, constitute as high as 20 to 30 per cent. The BJP's vision statement outlined a special economic package for the uplift of minorities. A change of heart was seen on the part of the mainstream party whose policies of communalism created chasm in the society. Gujarat pogrom is an example to substantiate this claim.

Addressing a rally in Muslim-majority Kishenganj (Bihar), Vajpayee said that the peace initiative taken with Pakistan was a 'proof that his Government never discriminated against anybody on communal lines'. "The peace process with Pakistan is good for Hindu-Muslim relation in the country," he said. This logic implies that if hostilities broke out between the two countries, Muslims in India would suffer the consequences.

Vajpayee tried to convince the minorities saying that the NDA Government had never used them as vote-bank and would continue with this attitude. "We believe in peaceful coexistence and the nation cannot be a theocratic nation," he said while addressing delegates at the BJP's Minorities Development Conference held before the elections. Promising to provide a proactive administration, he said his new dispensation would not allow anyone to die without food, medicine and hospital facilities.

Vajpayee said the minorities should think among themselves what was in their best interest. "We promise happiness through peace, progress and development," he exhorted and reminded them to give renewed mandate for the BJP. "A vote for the BJP is a vote for development, peace and progress and these are discernable as my administration has made them possible to a great extent," said Vajpayee in the meeting.

A Muslim *Yatra* to lobby for the BJP began in Lucknow. The *Yatra* members started to tour the state. Vajpayee asked them to tell the Muslims "not to nurse a feeling of being left out". Mentioning the India-Pakistan cricket tour of that time, he said there were some players who were Muslims. The *Yatra* was organised by a group of intellectuals who formed the 'Atal Behari Vajpayee Himayat Committee'. They included professors of universities, some *Imams* and former bureaucrats.

The BJP leadership offered several talking points to its cadres like "Never allow the Congress to deflect your attention and to focus on our failures. Give emphasis on development. Insist on a debate, the Congress' weak point. Compare 47 years of misrule of the Congress and five years of the BJP's performance. Tell the voters repeatedly: "You had given the absolute majority for the Congress at all levels, and you have seen what they had done on development front. You have given us a limited mandate; yet you have five years of good governance before you. We need stronger mandate to take up the developmental agenda forward."

The BJP leaders coined catchy slogans: *Shaktishali Bharat ke liye shaktishali Bhajpa*. "Think progressively, assert ideologically and campaign aggressively", the cadres were told repeatedly. The BJP cadres were asked to educate people about important issues like POTA, National Council for Educational Research and Training (NCERT) syllabus, dangers of infiltration, terrorism, scrapping of Illegal Migrants Determination Tribunal (IMDT) Act, need for anti-conversion law, ban on cow slaughter, interlinking of rivers, population control and need for providing reservation to economically backward people.

To mobilise public opinion Advani planned Bharat Uday Yatra in the run-up to the General elections. Announcing his plans for the *Yatra*, he said it had a 'conceptual and emotional link' to the Ram Rath Yatra of 1990 and the Swarna Jayanti Yatra of 1997, with a common thread of 'resurgent nationalism' running through all the three. The *Yatra*, he said, "captures the emerging reality and strengthening resolve of a resurgent India."

The *Yatra* was planned to cover 11,925 km over 32 days. Broken into two phases, it passed through 121 Lok Sabha constituencies from Kanyakumari to Amritsar, and Porbandar to Puri. Significantly it touched Ayodhya where Advani spent a night. The *Yatra* passed through the states where the BJP was yet to emerge as a major force. In his public addresses Advani showed off some clippings of unfinished projects and urged the voters to caste their votes in its favour, as a vote for BJP would make India a superpower. He attacked Sonia saying that she didn't belong to the country and had no understanding about India. He also flaunted for religious tolerance. He reminded the people that they had become prisoner of culture of negativism perpetrated by the Congress and the CPI (M). He felt proud that the BJP was able to harmonise the country's rich diversity and said that the party was committed to nationalism. He didn't fail to tell the people that improved India-Pakistan ties had brought Hindus and Muslims together.

Advani avoided tricky issues deliberately. On creation of Telengana, he said that it was not their agenda. He, however, advocated enforcement of two-child norm for jobs and public office and a fixed tenure for legislature.

In Maharashtra, he tried to present the party's liberal views saying atmosphere shouldn't be created to turn away the Muslim community, which would produce bad blood. He blamed the Congress that it had taken the community for a ride. He stressed that nothing would be done to alienate them. At several places he talked about his pet issue that was about the building of Ram temple. He promised to build it after the polls and also sought active cooperation of the Muslims in this regard. In Mathura he said that India would have a Ram Rajya and also claimed that congenial atmosphere had been prevailing for temple construction. He further claimed that India was shining but could shine much and termed the NDA Government as superb over Nehru's.

The *Yatra* was all about telling people that the BJP had given Suraj or good governance to the country. During the NDA tenure, good governance had been a constant Advani theme. He was saying that the elections would be all about good governance. Along with that, Advani believed that the *Yatra* would try to tap another emotion—that of nationalism.

During the NDA tenure, Sonia targeted the Government for its all-round failure to maintain social harmony, inability to provide national security or incapable to protect interest of the farmers. Since national security was among the BJP's main plank, Sonia touched a raw nerve in provoking its leaders to react to her allegations at a time when it was busy highlighting the Government's achievements.

Sonia criticised the Opposition severely for launching an attack on the country's composite culture. She said that it was evident in the form of state-sponsored carnage in Gujarat. Without naming the BJP, she said that the communal forces were out to denigrate the basic values of the Constitution.

"The author of the Constitution belongs to the broad-minded mainstream of our composite heritage. They rejected narrow chauvinism which characterises those who, in the name of their distorted vision of *Hindutva*, first enunciated the pernicious two-nation theory," she added. She said the country was confronted with great abyss in politics. "It separated those who believe in a composite tradition of nationhood from those whose theories of nationhood was based on narrow chauvinism and divisiveness".

It was Sonia's second parliamentary election after becoming Congress president. In her first election she was almost new to the hurly-burly world of electoral politics, though not the electorate. She needed some time to know all about politics. Now that she has learnt quite a lot about it, she takes elections seriously.

Sonia has learnt the essence of politics and the art of contesting elections very well. She has foresightedness and draws strategy well in advance. Travelling the length and breadth of the country in a hurricane election tour, Sonia caught the imagination of the masses by her emotional speeches in Hindi. It was noticed that she successfully adopted her mother-in-law's mannerism and style in influencing the large crowds, which turned up at her election rallies.

To reach out to the people the Congress party tried different stratagem. New styled snapshots of Sonia got ready for display in the Congress office. The stress was given on her 'Indianness'. Her mood, look and style were redefined. Look—Indian, mood—youthful, style—shining and smiling. The brain behind the photo-shots and her audio-video campaign were Salman Khurshid, Jairam Ramesh, Ahmed Patel, Ambika Soni, Pranab Mukherjee, Manmohan Singh and Arjun Singh. The party prepared an advertisement campaign showing Sonia as youth leader compared to Vajpayee.

OPINION AND EXIT POLLS

The NDA was over-sanguine that it would return to power. It began to consider the elections just a formality. All leading news channels and newspapers carried out surveys and opinion polls indicating its return. Even the astrologers predicted NDA's clear majority.

Besides doubts harboured by a section of the middle-class about Sonia's Italian origin, it was worth noting that she consistently secured an approval rating in the mid-20s in opinion polls in the question of becoming prime minister. Although she trailed behind Vajpayee, she was still ahead of big politicians in the list like Advani or Jyoti Basu, who notched up embarrassingly low single digit figures. Clearly there was not reluctance among the people to holding the coveted post by a 'foreigner'.

Sonia's high percentage might seem surprising despite the fact that she is politically inexperienced, lack of accessibility, deficiencies as a public speaker and inability to impart a sense of dynamism. Yet, sizeable proportion of the electorate still favoured her to be the prime minister next to Vajpayee and if the Vajpayee factor is put aside for a moment, she would be able to romp home easily. Since Advani scored 2 to Sonia's 26, as in *Outlook* magazine survey, it was patent enough that the *Lauh Purush* from Sindh was no match for the lady from Turin.

What this preference showed was that the voters were broad-minded enough to ignore the Italian background. It may also be due to the Indian view of the wife becoming so integral a member of the husband's family so as to obliterate her past lineage.

Sonia probably got an extra push as a member of the Nehru-Gandhi dynasty. As inheritor of Indira, she undoubtedly influenced the choice of the large number of women, especially in the rural areas.

Probably Vajpayee began to comprehend Sonia's popularity and that she was a threat for the BJP, so he raised the issue of her origin. He targeted Sonia's foreign origin for the first time at an election rally at Jawahar, Thane, in the state of Maharashtra and called for serious debate on whether a foreigner could occupy a high office in the country.

The Congress, however, accused Vajpayee of changing his stand of making the foreign origin a poll issue. The party had a valid reason to accuse him. In an interview in 1999 Vajpayee had said that he was not in favour of making the 'foreigner' issue a campaign plank, as that would not be a healthy issue for a public debate. Quoting from it, Congress wondered what had made Vajpayee say that Sonia's foreign origin was an issue that needed to be debated seriously. Vajpayee changed statements depending on the circumstances. The contradictory position taken in the past on major issues strengthened the belief that normally he didn't mean what he said.

On questioning Advani about the same issue he refused to be drawn to any controversy relating to Sonia's foreign origin, saying the Government had no obligation to review the issue. He said the Constitution Review Committee didn't consider the issue, so there was no need to pursue it again.

According to the survey, Vajpayee was 65 per cent better choice for the prime minister's post while Sonia is just 22. About Sonia's foreign origin, the survey found 55 per cent respondents opined that certainly it was an election issue. The survey also found that the BJP was best-placed to form the next government because 57 per cent respondents gave opinion in its favour while only 27 per cent thought the Congress had a chance to form the government.

PREDICTIONS

Many astrologers see elections as great opportunity to shoot into prominence. As the election process began they predicted which party would win and which party lose. They also predicted beforehand which party would get how many seats and who be the next prime minister.

Opinion polls, conducted in March-April by some news channels gave the BJP the magic numbers. Apparently influenced by the Government's 'India Shining' campaign, some astrologers predicted the outcome even before the parties had announced their list of the candidates.

Country's different news channels predicted results differently. The NDTV predicted 287 to 307 seats for the ruling alliance and 143 to 163 for the Congress-led alliance. Aaj Tak was more liberal in its assessment. According to its survey the NDA was to get anything 330 and 340 seats compared to the Congress' 105 to 115. Star TV gave 277 seats to the NDA and 164 seats to the Congress. Zee TV stopped sort of giving the NDA a majority, predicting 265 seats for the ruling alliance and 196 for the Congress. Sahara gave a marginal verdict, 271 for the ruling alliance and 168 for the Congress.

During elections, many more exit and opinion polls followed. Although some channels steadily whittled down the NDA majority but none got anywhere near the actual numbers.

SHOCK AND SURPRISE

The BJP-led NDA was sanguine of its return to power. Leading news channels and newspapers too indicated this possibility. And lo! When the results were out it was the Congress, which emerged victorious. The victory turned out to be a shock and awesome for many. The NDA looked on in utter disbelief, as if sky has fallen. All opinion polls proved wrong. Sonia with just six years of political experience was able to defeat the BJP headed by veterans Vajpayee and Advani. It was shocking that the BJP, which made a song and dance about a Vajpayee Vs Sonia election and considered her a trash, had to digest this reality.

Nobody in the Congress expected the party to emerge in a decisively strong position in the elections. The adverse circumstances under which she fought the elections needed mention. General assessment of the people, whether rural or urban, was that the BJP would return to power, perhaps with increased strength.

Sonia alone is the architect of the party's victory. By late March the manifesto and the vision statements were ready. She carried the entire burden of the campaign on her shoulder, travelling over 63,000 km and addressing more than 60 large public meetings throughout the country. This was apart from her *Jan Sampark Abhiyan*. The other senior leaders campaigned in their own states and those among them were fighting elections campaigned primarily in their own constituencies.

Compared to other news channels, the NDTV came closest after the last round of polls, saying the NDA would fall short by 22 to 42 seats. Taking the lower figure, (230), even they were off mark by over 40 seats. The assessment of the election results went terribly wrong. None of the pollsters reached anywhere near predicting that a Congress-led alliance would unseat the NDA Government nor did they project that the

Congress would win largest number of seats. They even underestimated the strength of the Left parties.

The Congress and allies together got 219 seats and the BJP and allies got 188. The Congress won 144 seats whereas the BJP got only 137. The Left Parties and others got 135 seats. The secular alliance performed much better in West Bengal, Kerala, Maharashtra, Bihar and Tripura.

The Congress emerged as the single-largest party, so its victory was complete and truly representative. In some states like Madhya Pradesh, Chhattisgarh and Rajasthan, where the party took the BJP head-on, the election results were not satisfactory and in states like Orissa, Karnataka, where it faced the BJP and its local allies, the Congress was virtually routed. Even in Maharashtra and Gujarat it managed only a close second. In West Bengal and Kerala, the Left decimated the Congress.

The election result sent shock wave in the BJP circles. Its leaders virtually became dumbfound. The BJP was finding it hard to accept that the voters had rejected the party and its mascot Vajpayee for greenhorn Sonia. While the party tried to blame the outcome on the failure of some of its key allies like the TDP and the AIADMK for failing to deliver the goods in their respective states, the bottom line was that the people had rejected the NDA for its failure on many fronts. If one message is derived out of the verdict was that the voters were dissatisfied with the NDA rule and so told it: "Enough of your rule for now. Please leave."

The joy and rapture among the Congress workers were virtually overflowing. The way thousands of them scrambled to greet their beloved leader is an indication how the people of the country perceive her persona as a leader. The scenes of exultation witnessed at 10, Janpath—so graphically captured on TV—moved the world to eulogize Sonia. The world leaders hailed Sonia for the stunning victory. US President George W. Bush saw it a victory of the Indian democracy. He said, "Once again we were shown how strong and how deep are the roots of Indian democracy." US envoy to India David C. Mulford expressed support to the new government and reminded that the US had a long relationship with the Congress. British Prime Minister Tony Blair hoped that India would remain a key ally. Bangladesh Prime Minister, however, gave full credit to Sonia saying that the Congress win was testimony to her leadership and the trust people reposed on her.

The BJP remained impervious to public opinion on Sonia's foreign origin. The party even refused to acknowledge Sonia's political and moral victory. Since its inception, the BJP came second to the Congress in three parliamentary elections that followed. In 1984, it opened account with just two seats. The BJP surpassed the Congress in the next three consecutive elections because then the party's command was not with the Gandhi dynasty. After Sonia became Congress President, the BJP got the break in its march.

Although the Congress party got more seats in 1999, it decided not to form government. Taking advantage of this, the BJP came to power. However, in the elections the BJP could not stand the impact of Sonia's rising popularity.

RESULTS AT A GLANCE

After Sonia's entry into politics, the Congress party maintained high percentage of votes. Her leadership ability and line of thinking were the plus points that made people vote for her. Another potent factor was her concern to uplift the weaker sections of the society. The party remained at the top in Parliament despite its number of seats falling in the Lok Sabha from 415 in 1984 to 114 in 1999. However, its vote share remained higher than the BJP's right through this period of decline. If the last three elections are taken into account, the Congress secured 22.88 per cent of votes in 1996, the year in which it lost power, 25.82 per cent in 1998 and 28.3 per cent in 1999. The BJP, on the other hand, got 20.2 per cent in 1996, 25.59 per cent in 1998 and 23.75 per cent in 1999. It was only in 1998 that the BJP nearly caught up with the Congress, but again fell behind to concede the number one position in terms of percentage the Congress had in 1999.

The basic reason for the progress was that the Congress reasserted its ideological position, emphasizing its commitment to pluralism, democracy, balanced economic reform, mindful of the need for distributive justice and a measured approach to problems of foreign policy and security based on an independent national approach.

Defeat for the media in these elections was even worse. The entire media got it horribly wrong as far as opinion polls are concerned. Almost six or seven polls were done by each of the major operators and no one was even remotely near the truth. They got the total for the NDA wrong by about 60 seats at the lowest. All except one got the Congress-plus figure wrong by around 40 at the highest.

Most importantly, no one predicted that the NDA would be lower than the Congress-plus. The media had clearly identified a winner (that is NDA) and right through the elections, its approach towards the Congress-plus was supportive.

A SUCCESSFUL LEADER

Sonia's record as Congress President is a saga of success despite the BJP ruling at the Centre. Many harboured doubts about Sonia's ability as a political leader. The doubts got cleared when the results of the elections came out. Even if the mandate was clearly against the ruling NDA Government (rather than for any particular party), it was pretty clear from the electoral arithmetic that the Congress had pulled off a big share and for this she deserves no small thanks.

The results prove that Sonia is a leader of exceptional ability. The qualities that a good leader should possess, she has all. She deserves acclamation for galvanizing the party that was not in good shape when she took over.

Due to her honest, fair, impartial and clean image, even her political foes have become friends. Being President of the largest political party, she knows her responsibility towards the nation. She is able to bring together all secular forces on the one side to free the country from communal grips. Although ideologically poles apart, she entered into alliance with like-minded parties forgetting past bitterness. Several left, right and centrist parties entered into tie-ups with her party. She held parleys with them and prepared a common agenda. All these parties have expressed confidence in her leadership.

The BJP's constant misinformation about Sonia hankering after power despite being a foreigner didn't work. If one goes through her public announcements over the last six years, not once did she say that she wanted to become prime minister. She always emphasised her commitment to the Congress and the country. This is what she said in an election rally, "I came into politics with a purpose to contribute what I could for the welfare of the people and to strengthen the party." Throughout the electoral campaign, she articulated the view that the Congress and its allies through consultation and consensus would decide the prime ministerial candidate.

The BJP leaders dubbed Sonia as 'reader' and 'just can't think on her own', but she has showed the world that she is far from it. Her party's victory over the BJP is proof enough that the years she spent in the Gandhi household were not spent in vain. Sonia is aware of the plight of the ordinary Indians, as she has travelled the remote areas of the country widely. It is her attachment and sense of duty, which makes her reach out to the people. Her entry into public life is not to seek any official position but to know the condition of the people and do what is good for them. She has devoted herself fully to the service of the country and its people without any return. By her selfless service it can be inferred that she is above greed and ambition. She has imagination and organisational skill. Her style of functioning is totally different. Even she utilises important days like birthday and new year day for the service of the people.

Birthdays are synonymous with greetings, party and gifts. Many people spend prodigious sum of money on the occasion to show off their influence in the society. But Sonia prefers to spend the day for public good. She spent her 60th birthday to express solidarity with the quake-hit victims of J & K. She visited the affected areas and met the injured children lacking treatment and got them shifted to Primary Health Certres and talked to people inside their homes to know their miseries. She saw for herself the progress of the construction and rehabilitation work and also had a look at the preparations made for the survivors ahead of the harsh winter months. She listened to people's complaints and as pragmatic she is, on the spot she instructed the state chief minister to make fresh assessment for their requirements.

Sonia first visited the area on October 10, 2005—two days after the quake hit the state. Then she promised the affected people to visit again. This visit was the fulfilment of her that promise. "I had promised the people that I would visit the area again. So here I am, among them all again. I have fulfilled that promise," she said. This act has lot of things to learn about her and that is: she has shunned materialism and gives importance to moral values. Through the visit one thing is reflected and that is what she promises, she tries to fulfil them.

Sonia's charismatic leadership has almost stopped people's flight from the party. After her entry into politics, there had been no deficiency of leadership. After Nehru, Indira and Rajiv, Sonia too is considered having the same personality with enormous mass appeal to win over people and bring in votes. Wherever she went, she attracted huge crowd. This is what she commands the kind of support she does.

Over the years Sonia has developed self-confidence. Her learning process is over. She has full control over the party. During her initial years as party President, the sceptics were doubtful about her ability to boost the image of the party. They used to sneer at her persona but now her acceptability among the masses has gone up enormously and the foreigner tag is no more a consideration among a vast section of the people.

Sonia has restored the confidence of the party leaders. Her authority is quite extensive and more widely acceptable. Congressmen rally round her out of instinct and it is her great strength. For her affability she finds a place in the hearts of the crores of people, so by that consideration she has become leader of the masses. As long as she enjoys the support of these leaders, she will rule over others.

Sonia is prepared to listen to all sorts of voices and has shown firmness in dealing with intra-party affairs. She means business and believes that those at the helm of affairs have to show their capability. They can't escape responsibility. That is why Congress government in the states are more stable and professionally run.

The fact is that Sonia was able to create a syndrome politically in the BJP camp. Besides, she had bravely taken on the BJP by attacking its 'communal' agenda and played an important role in defending secularism in the country, both in Parliament as well as outside.

As leader, Sonia uses authority when necessary and keeps the second-rung leaders under her command. She knows how to use the authority. She never hesitates to call a spade a spade. To substantiate this aspect, it is relevant to mention that she sent out several strong signals to show her discontent, including the one that she showed to Punjab Chief Minister Amarinder Singh when he dared to bypass the Prime Minister on the water sharing issue. Prime Minister was upset because he did not take into confidence either him or the party high command to enact the Punjab Agreements Termination Act. Punjab is involved in litigation with neighbour Haryana on the issue of sharing river water for over two decades. Amarinder later revealed that he didn't want to show disrespect to Prime Minister or anyone else. Punjab's interest was his uppermost concern.

Sonia is not a person to tolerate dubious role of the party leaders. When allegations came to her that Maharashtra Congress Committee chief Prabha Rau had indulged in imbalanced representation and 'sold' PCC posts, Sonia summoned her for an explanation. She also pulled up party in-charge of the state Margaret Alva for blindly endorsing whatever came from Rau.

Sonia represents a family that has sacrificed itself for the nation. Therefore, she has imbibed the values of courage and sacrifice from the family. She is the modern answer to the core issues that the Indian polity is facing. She has one mission and that is to serve people. This is what she said while addressing people in Orissa at the time of General elections: "I have not entered politics for power but for serving the poor and the downtrodden, which is the tradition of the Nehru-Gandhi families".

Sonia has taken many bold decisions that reflects her political maturity. The decision to form a coalition government with the PDP in 2002 gives enough indication of this. As a leader she has shown the nation that she doesn't hesitate to adjust with situation for greater public good.

Besides her Gandhi dynasty connection, Sonia herself has carved a niche that no one can dream of. It is absurd to say that a billion people have to look to foreign shores for political guidance. Some people blame the Congress that it couldn't come up with a credible political candidate. But what they fail to understand is that the dynasty has served the country for almost 40 years. No other leader in the country can boast of such a great feat.

Over the years Sonia's resolve has only grown firm. It is evident in her several speeches. She has pledged that the Congress party would concentrate on working at the grass-roots level to regain the confidence of the people.

Other political parties were blaming the Congress for every problem but Sonia never failed to give them befitting reply for the baseless charges. In reference to the attack on the minorities she said, "Communal and divisive forces" have become active in different parts of the country and called upon the people to remain watchful so that such forces wouldn't gain strength.

When party manifesto was being prepared Sonia played crucial role in it. She put forward for consideration such points that would help in uplifting the condition of the *aam admi*. The manifesto commits to provide free education to the deprived sections, from the primary to the university level. The party also promised to give women due representation in legislative bodies. As per the strategy of the party it already distributed a substantial member of seats to women in the last General Elections.

Sonia's victory was widely seen as a victory for her foresightedness. Being the President of the largest political party, she knows her responsibility towards the nation. To free the country from communal parties she entered into alliance with like-minded parties forgetting past bitterness. She held parleys with them and prepared a common agenda. All these parties expressed confidence in her leadership and also assured that they would not mind her becoming prime minister.

CROWNING MOMENT

After the Congress party's victory in the elections, it became almost clear that Sonia was going to be the country's next prime minister. Decks were cleared for her to become new prime minister as 145–member Congress Parliamentary Party (CPP) formally elected her leader in the Central Hall of Parliament. Veteran leader Pranab Mukherjee proposed her

Rahul greeting his mother at the CPP meeting

name while Manmohan Singh seconded it. Later addressing the gathering, she thanked her fellow party lawmakers saying, "You have honoured me by reposing your trust and faith in me. I feel deeply humbled. I feel greatly privileged." The text of her speech is produced below:

I stand here today, in the space once occupied by my greatest teachers, Panditji, Indiraji and Rajivji. Their lives have guided me throughout my journey. Their courage and complete devotion to India has given me the strength of continue on the path even years after their martyrdom. I would like to remember them today, I would like to honour them today.

We stand here as elected members of this august House as per the will of the people of our great nation. Let us never forget that it is to them we owe our positions. Let us not sleep, for even one moment. At all times, we must act in their interest, at all times we must acknowledge that it is their mandate that has given us this immense responsibility, at all times we must be conscious of the truth that we are, in fact, their humble servants.

Let us not revel our victory. Let us greet it as a welcome opportunity to effect the changes that may better the lives of our brothers and sisters all over India. Let us understand the sentiment behind this mandate. Let us each acknowledge that the people of India have chosen us to represent their aspirations, not our own. The people of India have spoken. They have once again reaffirmed what we have believed within our hearts. They have asserted that the soul of our nation is inclusive, secular and united.

They have decisively rejected the ideology of the likes of the RSS. They have decidedly rejected the destructive and self-serving policies of the BJP-NDA government. They have decidedly rejected the policies of personal attacks and negative campaign.

Very shortly a Congress-led coalition will be placed at the Centre. Even as we provide the pivot for the coalition, it will be our earnest endeavour to respect and work closely with our allies and partners. We will soon finalise a joint plan of action with them. This plan will outline our priorities, policies and programms as one cohesive unit.

The commitment to provide a strong and stable government dedicated to provide social harmony and peace unites all of us in a coalition. The commitment to provide a firm resolute government devoted to the welfare of the *kisans* and *khet mazdoor*, of youth and women, of weaker sections of society unites us all in the coalition. The commitment to provide a purposeful and effective government focused on accelerating employment growth and investment unites all of us in the coalition. We have an enormous task ahead of us. The road is wrought with difficulties, the challenges are vast. Let us not be complacent. Our party organisation has to be infused with new energy and drive.

In many states we have not performed as we should have. There is now a momentum generated by our revival—let us not squander it. We must utilize it as a catalyst for change and progress within our own organisation. I would like to extent my heartiest congratulations to each one of you and to express to you, my heartfelt gratitude. I am glad to see a number of young men and women who have joined the House today. A special word of greeting to them and a special thought for all those who fought hard but could not make it.

Altogether 18 parties were supporting her to form the government. Many of them extended their support in writing. With over 300 MPs in her kitty Sonia was set to meet President A.P.J. Abdul Kalam and stake claim to form the government. The Congress leaders were happy that their beloved leader would soon be seen seated at the constitutional top post for which they had been struggling for several years. In the meantime a suitable name was being considered for the new alliance, which would run the government. Several names were proposed but finally it was fixed on United Progressive Alliance (UPA).

As the time for the big event was approaching, there was jubilation among the Congress cadres all over the country. The cadres became restive to see their leader become prime minister who had come off with flying colours after making one of the most stunning electoral upsets ever against all odds. Moreover, she was in a position that no non-BJP leader had enjoyed since Rajiv's 1984 electoral victory.

Sonia was the Congress choice for the prime minister's post. It was also the unanimous decision of the allies too. Her name was proposed by DMK's M. Karunanidhi and seconded by RJD's Lalu Prasad and NCP's Sharad Pawar. Leaders of other parties like Left Front, Samajwadi Party and Rashtriya Lok Dal carried the proposal.

After supporting Sonia's candidature as prime minister, most Congress allies and its supporting parties reconciled themselves to the Congress electing a new leader to head the UPA government.

Even though Sonia was elected CPP leader two days back, whether she would become prime minister or not still remained unclear. There was wild rumour that Manmohan Singh, whom she considers a man of great integrity having been in various responsible positions, would be new prime minister. With this intention in mind the Congress chief had unscheduled meeting with alliance partners like Karunanidhi, Lalu, Surjeet, Paswan, Pawar and V.P. Singh ahead of another CPP meeting that evening. Coming out from her residence Lalu told waiting mediapersons that nothing had changed, it was Sonia who would be prime minister. According to him it was also decided that she would meet the President the next day to stake claim and allies would accompany her as a show of strength. However, some partners contested such decision saying that the allies shouldn't go with her as the President's invite was clearly for her only. Congress leader Pranab Mukherjee along with Manmohan Singh also addressed the mediamen saying that there was no scope for rumour, Sonia would be prime minister.

The allies barely left the 10, Janpath when again rumour started spreading. The Congress leaders waiting on the lawns for a word, there was talk that Sonia had changed her mind. The rumour spread quickly through TV channels. There was anxious moment for alliance partners once more. To gather facts, Lalu and some Left leaders rushed to 10, Janpath. This time she conveyed to them that on her becoming prime minister there might be protest over her foreign origin, that people might move court over it and that at the end she might prove to be a liability. Moreover, the NDA had already decided to boycott her swearing-in ceremony. She told the leaders unmistakably that she had accomplished what she had in mind to do—oust the NDA—and that now she had 'limited use' for power. The allies listened her to the end but refused to relent from their decision. They made the point that she wasn't just the leader of the Congress but of the newly formed alliance as a whole.

As planned, the next day Sonia met the President. Manmohan Singh was also with her. It was widely believed that she informed the President about the idea that was on her mind. Coming home she thought it was time to show what she had been telling the people about her purpose, that she never remained power hungry. At last she made up her mind to stick to her earlier decision not to occupy the prime minister's chair.

In the meantime the Left Front took decision to support the government from outside after all its constituents met. Earlier the Central Committee of the CPI (M) decided to provide outside support to the government. Other Left parties were discussing if they would join the government or not. The CPI (M)'s Central Committee again had a marathon discussion on the question of the party's role in the new government. The Left Front finally decided to support the government from outside only. The NCP and the DMK members were in two minds. After DMK Working Committee meeting, it decided to join the government. However, the NCP constituted a four-member team. Under its suggestion the party decided to join the government.

'STOP SONIA' CAMPAIGN

The very thought of Sonia becoming prime minister made people having leanings towards the Sangh Parivar see red. They refused to consider voting for her because she is Italian born and, therefore, a *Videshi*. Also they feared that when things would get tough, she might run away. Their argument was that she didn't want Rajiv to accept the career in politics, why should she consider doing the same for herself?

Even after the humiliating defeat, the BJP was harping on Sonia's foreign origin issue. She becoming prime minister was unbearable for most of the BJP leaders. Although a pall of gloom descended on the BJP camp, its leaders began to criticise the Congress for misleading the nation on its leadership issue. Some leaders made plans to stop this with all sorts of wild ideas. Then Madhya Pradesh Chief Minister Uma Bharti even said that the day Sonia be made prime minister, it would be the darkest day in the history of this country. She accused the Congress that it never projected Sonia as the prime ministerial candidate, so they had played guile with the electorate. Some BJP leaders worked out plans to stop her from becoming prime minister. The party also decided to boycott the swearing-in ceremony.

The latest offensive was entirely in line with the script that the BJP had followed since the election results were announced. As the party threatened to boycott the swearing-in ceremony, leaders like Sushma Swaraj and Uma Bharti created a disgusting situation. While Swaraj vowed to tonsure her head, Bharti staged a mock resignation drama. Not to be lagged behind, former BJP ideologue and RSS *Pracharak* K.N. Govindacharya emerged from his isolation to announce a nationwide Rashtriya Swabhiman Andolon (national self-respect campaign)." He said the real battle was against a section of the political class and intellectuals that allowed her to come close to occupying the top post. "We have to create awareness against this mindset. Sonia *per se* is not the main issue. What has to be fought is this arrogant mindset that considers the very repugnant thought of a foreigner becoming prime minister," he said.

The striking point was that not a single voice from the senior echelon of the party was raised against the sinister move perpetrated by the lower-rung leaders. Neither Vajpayee nor

Advani made honest efforts to put a stop to it. There was temptation within the party to blame the lack of *Hindutva* issues for its defeat in the election. The pragmatic knowledge was that such issues had lost their resonance with the electorate and that on close reading there were other causes to their defeat than a rejection.

Then Tamil Nadu Chief Minister Jayalalitha also raised the issue, saying Sonia with her Italian origin should not be allowed to become the prime minister of the country.

PARTIES' SUPPORT

Some parties, however, came in Sonia's favour. They are CPI (M), RJD, and LJP. Veteran CPI (M) leader Harkishan Singh Surjeet strongly defended Sonia saying that her foreign origin shouldn't come in the way of her leading a government. Even during electioneering Surjeet castigated the NDA leaders for making Sonia's foreign origin an election issue. "Nobody can debar her from taking up any post. The NDA leadership's attacks in this regard will have no impact as she enjoys the constitutional and legal right to take up any job, like any other Indian citizen," he said. Widely perceived as 'Chanakya' of Indian politics he said the NDA was harping on Sonia's foreign origin only to divert the people's attention from the real issues. It simply demonstrated the BJP's weakness and failures on all fronts, he said.

On the NDA leadership's plans to bring legislation to debar persons of foreign origin from holding high office, once Surjeet quipped, "Where have they been for 55 years? Ours is a democratic country and not a dictatorship. This is all the more important to ensure their defeat at the hustings. We are now supporting the Congress despite the fact that we have differences with them on economic issues...it is in the paramount interest of the nation today that the NDA is ousted, as its continuance in power will endanger our social fabric and unity in diversity. The BJP's continued campaign on foreign issue is bound to boomerang on it as communal policies never pay in the long run."

INNER VOICE

The Congress leaders became impatient to see Sonia take oath as prime minister. But in reality she was in two minds—about whether she should stick to her own pledge by not accepting the top post or make her supporters happy by becoming the prime minister. She hears an inner voice. It tells Sonia to decline the prime minister's post. This voice puts her almost in a state of indecision for two days, most of the time pensively weighing pros and cons whether to become prime minister or not. The senior party leaders couldn't make how to win over her. They felt dejected for her stand to relinquish the top post.

As word spreads about Sonia's decision to step aside, a section of her party leaders still hoped that she would allow herself to be persuaded. The only informed people in the prevailing confusion were her close aides and associates. In fact, her decision to summon the newly elected MPs to a tea party just a day after her election as CPP leader was the real motive behind the scene.

Originally Sonia had planned to withdraw her candidature before responding to President Kalam's invite for a meeting but she put her plans on hold under pressure from the Congress allies who had elected her leader of the UPA. She didn't press the issue as allies like Lalu and Paswan made out a strong case for not being browbeaten by the Sangh Parivar. They argued that as the leader of the new formation, she shouldn't be acting unilaterally.

Sonia was primarily responsible for rejuvenating the secular front. In retrospect, it appeared that the pressure on her was much more from within her family that the 'secular alliance' which she had formed made all out effort to forestall the BJP's return to power. Her children, worried about the possible threat to her from the fanaticism, were not forthcoming about what their mother should do.

At last the scale tilted in favour of her, giving up the prime ministership. The letters of support from the UPA constituents were ready when Sonia left 10, Janpath for Rashtrapati

Bhawan for the second time. But she chose to leave the letters behind. That was the first indication of the path she had chosen. "I will meet the President again with the support leaders," she told the waiting reporters after the meeting.

Sonia instructed her political secretary Ahmed Patel and other senior leader to convey her stand to the allies: "Tell them I am not going to reverse my decision." In the evening the CPP meeting was convened. Senior leaders were deputed to carry her messages to Surjeet, Lalu, Paswan and several others. Prominent among her emissaries were Manmohan Singh, K. Natwar Singh, Arjun Singh, M.L. Fotedar, Ahmed Patel and Ghulam Nabi Azad.

"The post of prime minister is not my aim. My inner voice tells me that I decline the post," with these words Sonia announced before the CPP her decision not to accept the top post. She didn't name any party for her taking such a decision although there was a vicious campaign against her such wish.

The announcement drew protest from her party leaders as expected. They didn't want to listen anything and began to interrupt her again and again. The meeting was marked by emotions, high drama and protests. The speech she made is as under:

> Throughout the past six years that I have been in politics, one thing has been clear to me and that is as I have often stated that the post of prime minister is not my aim. I was always certain that if ever I found myself in that position that I am in today, I would follow my own inner voice. Today, the voice tells me I must decline the post. You have unanimously elected me your leader, in doing so you have reposed faith in me. It is this faith that places me under tremendous pressure to reconsider my decision. Yet, I must abide by the principles, which have guided me all along.
>
> Power itself has not attracted me, nor has the position been my goal. My aim has always been to defend the secular foundation of our nation and the poor of the country—the creed sacred to Indiraji and Rajivji. We

> have moved forward a significant step towards that goal. We have waged a successful battle but we have not won the war. That is a long and arduous struggle, and I will continue it with full determination.
>
> But I appeal to you to understand the force of my conviction. I request you to understand my decision to recognize that I will not reverse it. Our foremost responsibility at this critical time is to provide India with a secular government that is strong and stable.
>
> Friends, you have given me your generous support; you have struggled against all odds with me. As one of you and as President of the Congress party, I pledge myself to work with you and for the country. My resolve will, in fact, be all the more firm, to fight for our principles, for our vision and for our ideals.

After she had finished, the leaders took the microphone one by one for close to three hours to implore her to stay.

In identical voice the leaders said: "The votes the party got were the votes for you, so Madam, please don't go."

It didn't help. Sonia asked her colleagues "to understand the force of (her) conviction" and to recognise that she would not reverse her decision. At the end of the meeting she told party leaders that if they trusted her they should allow her to take decisions.

PREDICAMENT

The CPP meeting ended with no decision on who would replace Sonia as the alliance's prime ministerial candidate. Nor was there any word on the subject till late at night. There were, however, indications that Sonia wanted Manmohan Singh as the next prime minister.

To keep the alliance intact, even Rahul and Priyanka got a couple of phone calls. One amongst those who talked to them was Paswan. He told Priyanka and Rahul to persuade their mother to revise her decision. But that was not to be. Sonia withstood pressure both from her party leaders and allies, urging them to trust her and let her decide the leadership question.

In the meantime, West Bengal's veteran CPI (M) leader Jyoti Basu tried to clear the prevailing doubts about Sonia' unwillingness to accept the post of prime minister. He quoted Rahul and Priyanka as saying that they had lost their father, so they didn't want to lose their mother. He said no one could give them any assurance.

It was one of the extraordinary moments in the history of Indian politics—so to say in the history of India's parliamentary democracy. Sonia, who single-handedly took on the BJP-led NDA and trounced it, though widely perceived as the next prime minister refused to become so. The NDA leaders may be happy but the stand she took made it look foolish.

Sonia had made it clear through several interviews and public meetings that she was not in politics to become prime minister. She was in it with a sense of duty and not because of ambition. In this country the people's general perception is that most politicians want to reach at the top. This didn't apply to her and this is what makes her different from the others.

Sonia knew that there would be unprecedented protest against her decision but was prepared to face the aftermath. She remained firm to fight for the values she believed in—a secular India where people are not judged on the basis of religion or caste. If she had fought the battle on the BJP's terms, it would have been an admission to defeat before the struggle was actually over.

Pondering over the entire gamut of her political future, she made up her mind not to give in to colleagues' pressure and firmly decided not to become prime minister. Her decision sent shock waves across the country. There were spontaneous protest and demonstrations, roadblocks and self-immolation bids against her decision. But she remained unmoved.

Sonia's decision not to accept the prime minister's post put the Congress cadres in a tizzy all over the country. They demonstrated their devotion to the Gandhi family and made it clear that they couldn't accept anyone else as leader.

In New Delhi the scene was hysteric. The Congress workers thronged the residence of Sonia urging her to revoke her decision. The excitement was so high that senior party leaders were moved and hooted by the party cadres. "Sonia has our confidence. Sonia or nobody," they shouted.

The Congress workers campaigned outside 10 Janpath. Even though a feeling of resignation that she was firm in her abdication of the prime ministership sunk, they kept the decibel level in expressing their loyalty for her and insisting that no one else was acceptable.

"*Khali kar do raste, Soniaji ke vaste* (make way for Sonia)," shouted youth cadres repeatedly, daring anyone to suggest otherwise. Their rage was so high that a TV journalist was roughed up while he was speaking of possible alternative to a cadre. The cadres also vent their ire at the Congress headquarters. Some called her reluctance to accept prime ministership as 'unreasonable', others said she had no right to withdraw. That view was strongly echoed by many supporters.

"*Unki marji nahin chalegi* (her own wish is irrelevant). People have voted for the Congress because of her. She will have to heed the inner voice of the people, not her own," they argued. "The mandate is for her and not Manmohan. She must respect it," they said.

Ardent Sonia loyalists took to theatrics to convey their plea. One loyalist stole the show by climbing atop a parked vehicle and putting a revolver to his forehead. He threatened to suicide—truly filmy style—if Sonia didn't accept prime ministership. This lasted 15 minutes after which police were able to disarm him. Another party cadre climbed on a tree outside the rear entrance of Sonia's residence.

Not to be left behind, Mahila Congress workers signed appeals to her in blood. "Sonia or suicide" threatened a placard. Effigies of Sushma were burnt by the angry mob. Slogans were also raised against Bharti. The police had to cordon off the area around Sonia's residence and blocked the traffic as party members squatted on Janpath and Akbar Road in their resolve to get her to change mind. With media people descending in hordes, the scene gradually assumed the air of a carnival and Rajasthani folk artists arrived on the scene to entertain all.

The Congressmen began to feel that Sonia's abdication was discouraging. They considered Manmohan Singh as an educated man but their wish was that Sonia must be prime minister. With Sonia sticking to her decision, it discouraged the demonstrators very much. Same situation prevailed throughout the country.

In Varanasi, police foiled an attempt by some Congress activists to self-immolate themselves.

In Pondicherry the Congress legislators threatened to resign en masse if Sonia wouldn't accept prime minister's post.

In Guwahati, the Congress workers came out in the open and blocked Guwahati-Shillong road.

In Lucknow the Congress activists sat on hunger strike in front of the party office.

In Hyderabad over 500 Congress activists torched Sushma's effigy for her remarks on Sonia.

However, in Bhopal a Shiv Sena leader tried to immolate to protest against Sonia becoming prime minister.

Rare is the Indian politician who turns away from position when it was offered to him or her on a platter. Sonia is now the only person in Indian history to have turned down the post of prime minister not just once but thrice. The first time Sonia declined the top office in 1991 when the party returned the power at the Centre. It was so probably because she was in mourning. Moreover, she was not a political person. The second time was in 1999 when it seemed like the Congress might form the government. She had even let the then President know her stand. Manmohan Singh was her choice for the post that time. This time round, however, the circumstances were entirely different. Sonia not only heads the party but had fought and won elections.

The Congress leaders Manmohan Singh, Arjun Singh and Ghulam Nabi Azad met the Left leaders at Surjeet's residence. Emerging from a meeting, CPI (M) politburo member Yechuri said, "Our stand before the election was that we would accept whosoever the Congress elects as its leader. We have now been told (by the Congress leaders) that the party will now elect a new leader."

Earlier Jyoti Basu, who met Sonia twice before the Left decided to provide outside support to Congress-led government, said: "Who the Congress elects its new leader is that party's internal matter; we will accept their decision." Like Basu, Chatterjee said, "The Congress decision to elect a new leader was an internal matter," hinting that "the Left was not against seeing Manmohan Singh head the Government, our support is for secular party".

The Left Front (LF) didn't appeal to Sonia to reconsider her decision to withdraw from the race. The Samajwadi Party (SP), the Jharkhand Mukti Morcha (JMM) and the Bahujan Samaj Party (BSP) also said they would continue to support the Congress even if it chose a new leader.

Though the SP and BSP had not integrated with the 'secular' alliance, they had no option but to join the alliance as they too were wedded to the principle of secularism.

SP's Amar said: "It is an internal matter of the Congress. the SP has given its support to the Congress and not to any individual."

JMM's Soren said: "We will accept any person as prime minister whom Sonia chooses."

Reacting to his mother's decision not to accept the prime minister's post, Rahul said, "I can firmly say that no one in India could have taken such a decision. I would not have been able to do so." Priyanka reacted thus: "What she has done is in keeping with the rich Indian culture and tradition."

MANMOHAN FINAL CHOICE

After refusal to become prime minister Sonia announced the name of experienced, highly qualified and honest leader

Manmohan Singh for that post. Although remorse for not able to make their beloved leader become prime minister, the loyal Congress leaders accepted her decision with all humility. Later Manmohan was nominated leader of the CPP while she became Chairperson of it. For the Chairperson post the CPP constitution was amended. A resolution was passed giving her power to nominate leaders of the Rajya Sabha and the Lok Sabha.

Sonia then made a statement committing herself to the party and asking her party leaders to give their unstinting support to Manmohan Singh. "I am not going anywhere. I am still very much in politics. I will continue as Congress President and Chairperson of the CPP as long as you want me to," she said.

When Sonia spoke, she expected that there would be some disappointment and sadness because most people wanted her only to be prime minister. She was totally overwhelmed by the outpouring of emotions that were shown from nearly all parts of the country. "I have been humbled by the love and affection that were spontaneously expressed. To all of you who are upset or disappointed I have this to say: I am not going anywhere. I am still very much in politics. I will continue as Congress President and Chairperson of the CPP for as long as you want me to. I am one of you and nothing will ever change that," she said.

Sonia went on to say: "I entered politics out of a sense of duty and commitment. My family has always treated politics as part of a crusade to create a better India. Indiraji and Rajivji made supreme sacrifice for our nation. Their examples inspired us all and speaking for myself, I know that I derive my strength from their courage. No matter how much adversity I have faced, it is nothing compared to what they had to go through. Today, it is their strength and their inspiration that guide the Congress party and me. I understand your disappointment. But I appeal to you to understand the depth of my sentiment, when I say that I can't reverse my decision. We live in times when politics is about power. Let us show the world that for the Congress party, politics is about values and about integrity, I am overwhelmed by your love. But now, we must get on with the serious business of undoing the damage done by the last government and of working to create the India of our dreams."

Sonia urged the Congressmen to support the prime minister and give full support to the new cabinet. She said, "The Congress party is overwhelming with talent. Let us give India the government it deserves. Speaking for myself, I will always be here, working for the party. The Congress is my life. All of you are my family. Let us now build the 21st century India that was Rajiv's vision."

Later Manmohan Singh went to Rashtrapati Bhawan to stake claim to form the government. The President invited him. The swearing-in was fixed for Saturday, May 22.

Sonia's decision not to take the top job even after her spectacular election victory may have been her best-kept secret but her faith in Manmohan Singh was something that was widely known. The soft-spoken Sikh, who was responsible for pulling the economy from its worst crisis in 1991, was expected to be the finance minister in Sonia's cabinet. Instead, he emerged as the prime minister of her choice. One of the important reasons why he was chosen for the prime minister's post was because it was he who coined the phrase, "Liberalisation with a human face."

After Sonia stunned the nation by refusing the power that came to her on a platter, Rahul said that his mother acted just as a true Gandhi would. "My mother is not a Gandhi by blood...but yes! She became one. I would not be able to act the way she did," Rahul said and added that he felt proud of his mother. "I have seen my grandmother take oath as prime minister in 1980 and my father in 1984. I didn't feel as proud then as I felt when my mother refused to be prime minister."

Rahul and Priyanka knew the biggest story beforehand. Rahul said, "After the elections, on the day I collected my certificate, I asked my mother whether she wanted to be prime minister and she told me that she didn't."

GREAT RENUNCIATION

By her renunciation Sonia has become a hallmark of great sacrifice in the pages of history. Many questions arise from her refusal to accept the top post, a position that was legitimately hers from the political, constitutional and electoral points of view.

By giving up the country's top post, Sonia's magnanimity reached the zenith. People began to call her saint. Her decision was acclaimed internationally. Thus she set an example in the history of Indian democracy. By her act she introduced a distinct kind of politics in the country.

Since Mahatma Gandhi refused to lead Independent India's first government, no other leader had made so great an act of renunciation. Sonia's decision not to become prime minister stunned the whole country. The NDA, which had geared itself to launch a highly xenophobic attack on her, only watched in disbelief. Sonia's act of renunciation had destroyed NDA's strategy and exposed the BJP's power-hungry nature.

By declining the prime ministership for the third time Sonia acquired a stature that very few leaders in the world may have attained. She showed that it was not position for which she entered public life. It was her commitment to the poor, downtrodden and weaker sections that became weightier than her personal position.

By shunning power Sonia, whose overall rating in the opinion polls before the elections were below Vajpayee's, left him far behind. In fact, Vajpayee's silence over the manner in which Sushma, Uma and company were raising the foreign origin issue had added nothing but subtracted from his overall image.

By refusing the prime minister's post, Sonia emerged as Congress President with clout bigger than that of any other leaders. About her firm belief, she has shown that once a thing is decided, there is no scope to change it. Any amount of persuasion won't be able to weaken her conviction. What she has shown, can be lesson for the future politicians. However, she has put an end to the issue of her foreign origin once and for all.

Ever since Sonia announced her decision, speculation had been rife about what made her take this decision. The NDA's spokesman hastened to claim it as a victory for its principled stand that no person, not born an Indian, should ever become the prime minister. They also chided her for insulting the nation by making 'light' of such an important position and misleading the nation into thinking that she wanted to become prime minister when she had no such intention.

A few years ago Sonia story could only end one way—retreat rather than glory. Barring the family name, there was little that ran in her favour. She was alien in every sense of the term. But that Sonia is a different material nobody knew. During the election campaigning she never projected anyone for the prime minister's post. She didn't divulge to anyone her decision to renounce prime ministership till she was elected CPP leader mainly to hold the party together as well as to ensure that the allies wouldn't withdraw support if she announced her plan in advance.

It was not the fear of physical violence that led Sonia to take a decision to renounce prime ministership. There may be some element of influence by her children, but it could not have been decisive. Basically what she said in the Central Hall of Parliament while announcing her decision was valid. The 'inner voice' or conviction that led her to the decision was an expression of her approach to politics—that individual is not more important than the party.

Besides Indian media, Nepali and Sri Lankan press hailed Sonia for her renunciation of the prime minister's post and urged the local politicians to see her as a role model. *The Rising Nepal* said "her renouncing office provides a lesson to countries in the region that are embarrassingly soaked in the power game". It further said, "Nepali leaders must learn from Indian politics...and struggle for democracy, not power." Lanka's *Daily Mirror* said, "It requires great courage and determination...to sacrifice personal glory and privilege for one's country's larger interests. This indeed is a quality of leadership that is woefully lacking in the leaders of this country."

The New York Times termed Sonia's decision of not accepting the prime minister' post as 'sensible'.

MANMOHAN IN THE SADDLE

The swearing-in of the UPA Government headed by Manmohan Singh was held on May 22. The UPA comprises 19 parties and Sonia is the Chairperson of it. It was a gigantic task for her to keep all the partners happy while allocating the portfolios. Many of them even made her know of their choices beforehand but she is something else. In allocating portfolios, the Congress seemed to have had an upper hand. It refused to concede to the demands of specific portfolios made by alliance partners, including the NCP's Pawar, RJD's Lalu Prasad and LJP's Paswan. None of the key alliance leaders really got what they wanted. Reportedly keen to get back Defence portfolio he once held, Pawar settled for Agriculture and Food after the Congress made it clear it wouldn't part with ministries of Home, Defence, Finance and External Affairs. This, in effect, also nipped Lalu's dreams of heading the Home Ministry, which the BJP's Advani presided over. The RJD chief then decided to head the Rail Bhawan. His gains, however, raised Paswan's hackles. The LJP leader, who was eying this ministry, went into a deep sulk. It took the persuasive skills of AICC leader Ahmed Patel and Sonia's personal intervention before Paswan relented on the stand articulated by his supporters: *Rail nahin to oath nahin*.

The muscle flexing by the allies gave Manmohan Singh first taste of running a coalition even as he and Sonia literally burnt midnight oil to iron out the irritants while hammering out the Congress-led cabinet. After 11 hours of marathon meeting, the exercise of placating allies continues for two days. Paswan finally came on board barely two hours before the swearing-in.

The failure of some of the allies to get what they wanted is not likely to prevent them from putting pressure on the

Congress on other issues at a later date. Sonia personally called up or interacted with allied leaders through her emissaries. She also took the initiative to personally inform and congratulate the Congress leaders about their inclusion in the cabinet.

Sonia's gesture touched many, especially after she declined the prime minister's post. Some party leaders offered to opt out of the government to work with her in the party. Former AICC general secretary Ambika Soni, senior party leader Subodh Kant Sahay and National Council for Women Chairperson Girija Vyas are some of them. Soni, who was tipped to join the Government as a cabinet minister, chose to stay out. In a letter to the Congress President, Soni sought permission to 'emulate' her. "I too would like to work with your motto of selflessness and service to the nation," she said expressing the hope that Manmohan Singh "will welcome it". However, Soni joined the Government later. Vyas was greatly influenced by Sonia's gesture. In fact, Vyas said that three women had shaped her destiny and they are her mother, Indira and Sonia.

Many believed that Soni didn't join the Government because she wasn't getting the portfolio she wanted. When she was quizzed about it she replied, "The question is not fair to me." The reference was about speculation that she had wanted the rank of a cabinet minister in the Prime Minister's Office (PMO), which was not possible.

A PERSON OF PRINCIPLE

Sonia is an icon among the present politicians. She is a stalwart in any pitch and a nationalist to the core. She always measures values from the angle of the people's welfare. She is a person of principle and doesn't compromise with it in spite of fear of losing something. She keeps her image clean at any cost. She is a good-hearted person, always ready to sacrifice for the country's good. She is a rebel against the social inequality.

By making Manmohan Singh the Prime Minister, Sonia hasn't freed herself from the pressures and demands of the coalition partners. She discharges her responsibility well and intervenes when such situation comes and gives directions to that effect.

In the hours when Congressmen were demonstrating outside her house and pleading with her in the Central Hall of Parliament to change her mind, seasoned analysts felt that this was no more than a political ploy to rally street power behind her in the struggle that lay ahead. When she refused to change her mind, some speculated that she had been overwhelmed by an attack of panic, while those of pro-BJP leanings attributed that the President had refused to swear her in because of a list of alleged irregularities that he wanted her to clear up first.

Mercifully, the President's office denied that it had questioned Sonia about her citizenship. President Kalam didn't raise the issue of Sonia's citizenship when the latter met him to discuss the government formation, a press release issued by the President's Press Secretary S.M. Khan said dismissing as 'contrary to facts' media report that Kalam was believed to have sought certain clarifications regarding Sonia's Indian citizenship. "I led the campaign for the Congress party, the people voted for the Congress led by me, so I don't think this was ever an issue," she replied when her reaction was sought over the gossip.

These speculations revealed more about the values and aspirations of the speakers than they did about the Congress President. The simple truth is that the episode would go down in history as the day when people saw the best that the Indian politics can produce and certainly her act would inspire the next generation of politicians.

Sonia's explanation of her action was disarmingly simple: She had never coveted the post of prime minister. She had entered into the fray to defend the secular foundation of the nation and to uplift the conditions of the poor of the country. With the alliance's victory the country has certainly moved a significant step towards that goal.

Sonia has learnt very well the art of handling and interacting with the mediapersons. She has come a long way since her entry into the public life. She is no more media shy and has the gift of the gab in replying questions. The weighty and curt reply she sometimes gives is an indication of this. Her wit and candour were witnessed when she fielded questions at the Hindustan Times Leadership Summit. Her understanding of the subject and presentation of the same in deftness was appreciated by many.

During campaigning the way she wooed the middle-class without alienating the poor sections is really wonderful. It is a tough call even for a seasoned politician. Given the contradictions and complexities of Indian politics, she has the aptitude to subvert the rival's plans. Her approach to the neglected class is very convincing.

Sonia believes that success in tackling one challenge would help in dealing with the other. As the Congress' secular credentials distinguish it from the BJP, the attack on the BJP-RSS ideology and the BJP-NDA's mis-governance acted as a cementing bond for the UPA that was forged on an anti-BJP plank. The Congress is of the view that the BJP practises politics of hate, which is why the Congress has no meeting ground with it.

A leader is made; no one is a born leader. She has enormous leadership ability. This outlook about her has begun to change in the BJP camp also. Some of its leaders have recognised her extraordinary leadership ability. Vajpayee's remark made in 2002 purportedly about her understanding and ability that "she is a woman and that too a foreign woman" now doesn't hold water. The party's senior leader Shatrughan Sinha considers her influence in the party in a different way. Judging her authority in the party for quite a long time, now he doesn't hesitate to call her a 'lady of substance' and a 'one-man army'. "If I praise Sonia, it is because she is lady...a lady of substance. Moreover she comes from tremendous background—Jawaharlal Nehru, Indira Gandhi and Rajiv Gandhi. She is a great fighter, a great survivor. I call her one-man army of the Congress, not one-woman, but one-man army of the Congress," he said about her.

Bollywood superstar Shahrukh Khan also expressed similar view about Sonia. In an interview to CNN-IBN's *Devil's Advocate* programme, he said, "There is an image of her that I would like to repeat again and again—on the bus, on an election rally and with children—which is a strong emotion to me as I am attached to the figure of a mother. For me she is a strong lady, someone you can admire." When asked if he had any ambition to enter into politics, he said that his idolising of the Congress President stemmed out of his admiration and had no political connotation. "When I said Sonia is a wonderful person, I said it quite apolitically," he said.

The RSS mouthpiece *Organiser* also praised Sonia's leadership and the way she runs the UPA Government. In an editorial it said, "Sonia Gandhi has stepped into husband's shoes. Her stern chiding of sycophancy has surprised everybody." It further said that she aggressively confronted and fought with the Left parties to defend the policies pursued by the Congress-led UPA Government.

Sonia works hard to keep the party in order and driving the country towards the path of progress. After the glorious victory in the General elections, she has effected changes in the AICC set-up several times. The only message she wants to send to the new team was that performance would be the only criterion for securing a place in either the party or the government.

Sonia is a strong believer in democracy and always tries to follow the democratic norms. This is evident in her style of functioning. Decisions are taken keeping in mind greater perspective of the situation in the country. She believes that the BJP is nothing more than an extension of the RSS the aim of which is to see India as a 'Hindu Rashtra'.

To make the organisation function better, Sonia bring changes in the party functionaries from time to time. On the basis of previous performance she retains some and inducts some who can help in inculcating new ideas in the establishment. Although sometimes there is mixed reaction over the allocation of work but nobody goes against her decision and accepts the responsibility with great humility.

Sonia is the nucleus and other functionaries are picked up on the basis of their utility. She allocates responsibility but also summons them for any anomaly. She is of firm view that when responsibility is taken, it has to be discharged properly. That is why she organises conclaves and asks her chief ministers for a progress report.

RANK AND HONOUR

The globally reputed magazine *Forbes* named Sonia as the world's third most powerful woman in 2004. The magazine in its citation said, "No other woman in the recent times has been more widely revered in India than Sonia."

The magazine's classification was about women who were changing not only societies where they work but also the role of women in power.

The *Forbes* ranking for Sonia is no doubt her personal achievement but it has instilled pride among the countrymen, particularly the Congress supporters. The noteworthy point is that she achieved this rank in just six years after entering active politics. In such a short period she established herself so solidly in the party that she becomes synonymous with the Congress and the Congress with her. Sonia's achieving of third rank is something spectacular and for this her persona deserves accolades.

Reaching this height was not so easy for the Congress chief. When she took the command of the party it was in a state of decline. Her becoming President of the party worked like an elixir. In the first few years she acquainted herself with the problems faced by the party and the country by organising conclaves at different levels. She was constantly receiving feedbacks by interacting with the district and the block-level activists. She had been monitoring the performance of the Congress-ruled states and corrective measures taken from time to time. The result was that the party began to fast regaining lost grounds. In five years her party was ruling half the country even though the BJP-led NDA ruled at the Centre. One remarkable thing about her was the ability to create fear psychosis in her rival camps. She always remained the centre of attack by them.

Sonia fits the *Forbes* references to the T. No doubt, she has emerged as the most distinguished and capable politician of the present times. The respect and the reverence she enjoys, the power and the position she holds and the commands and controls she wields in the party as well as in running the central and state governments are pre-eminent. The way she single-handedly propelled the party to power at the Centre is certainly a great accomplishment on her part.

Sonia was honoured 'The Guardian's Women of the Year, 2004' award. She shared the honour with a galaxy of global women personalities such as Condoleezza Rice, Kelly Holmes, the British Double Gold winning athlete, and Margaret Hassan, the modern-day nightingale, who lost her life while serving the Iraqis as an aid worker.

The British daily described Sonia's decision to decline prime minister post as simply flabbergasting. That decision was probably the first recorded example of a politician with humility, the daily observed. It quoted from Sonia's speech to shower fulsome praise on her as the great woman personality of the year.

This is what the editors of *The Guardian* had to say on why and how they decided to include Sonia in year-end honours. "That Sonia won the Indian General elections was surprising enough. That she turned down the post of prime minister was simply flabbergasting. In May, the 57-year-old Italian widow of former Prime Minister Rajiv Gandhi looked set to become India's next prime minister. Nearly 380 million people voted in the election, many of those turning out to vote for Gandhi's Congress party being the nation's poor."

Congress party's win was the fitting sequel to Sonia's year of exertion. It is an achievement for which she has to be proud. Undoubtedly, she deserved to get such honours as she worked hard to make her party win, which was well-nigh impossible under the prevailing circumstances.

The latest and most noteworthy honour bestowed on Sonia was by Belgian Government in recognition of her constructive nationalism. Belgian Prime Minister, Guy Varhofstadt, conferred on her the honour, the Grand Officer of the Order of Leopold, one of the three Belgian national honorary orders and the highest military order, named after King Leopold I. Explaining the situation for being a European woman leading the governing party of the world's largest democracy she fondly recalled her marriage to Rajiv Gandhi and said what she was today was largely because of being a member of "the remarkable family" into which she married and the love she received from the people of India. On the occasion she said, "I am reminded of what my mother-in-law, Mrs Indira Gandhi, used to say—one's real education is in the university of life. What I am today is largely because of being a member of the remarkable family into which I married, and because of the love I have received throughout from the people who have accepted me as their own."

The Congress President was also conferred honorary doctorate "Honorus Causia" of Vrije Universiteit Brussels (VUB)—Free University of Brussels. She received the degree from Professor B Van Camp, Rector of VUB. Receiving the honour Sonia addressed the gathering in the following words, "I am truly overwhelmed by the singular honours you have bestowed upon me. I do believe that by conferring these distinctions, you are recognising not the individual that I am, but the values I have imbibed and stand for."

Sonia also inaugurated Tejas, an exhibition of Indian art, showcasing sculptures dating from the Third Century BC to the 12th Century AD at the Palais Des Beaux Arts (BOZAR), the first exhibition of its kind and magnitude outside India. Delivering speech on the occasion she said, "Tejas symbolises the enduring dynamism and creativity of Indian culture. It projects India's civilisational journey over 1500 years of a most formative period of its past. The Indian civilisation is an inclusive one. Over the centuries, it has absorbed influences, faiths, ideas and peoples, without compromising its essential integrity and strength. Today, our nation is a land of diversity and variety on a continental scale. Though outwardly there was diversity and infinite variety among our people, everywhere there was that tremendous impress of oneness, which had held all of us together for ages past, whatever practical fate or misfortune had befallen us. India is the birthplace of four major religions and home to the second largest population of yet another faith, Islam. India welcomed Christianity long before Europe as well as the followers of Zoroastrian and Jewish faiths."

Sonia also paid tribute to thousands of unknown India soldiers at Ypres, the west Flanders region about 130 km from Brussels, who fought and fell in World War I at the Menin Gate, the route the soldiers took towards fighting the white man's war. The losses were heavy, estimated to be around 43,000 to 65,000. She wrote a message in the Book of Honour of the Last Post Association (LPA), quoting the 19th century American poet Emily Dickinson: "My being here to pay homage to the brave Indian soldiers who laid down their lives in the prime of their youth and so far away from beloved motherland reminds me of the poet's line, 'It feels a shame to be alive when men so brave are dead, one envies the distinguished dust, permitted such a head'. I salute their memory". Bugle calls the soldiers' ultimate sacrifice at 8 O'clock every night for 80 years. President of LPA, Benoit Mottrie, extolled the sacrifices of Indian soldiers in the darkest days of their history and said each day Flemish people remember the soldiers.

SAVIOUR OF DISTRESS

Sonia endeared herself to the people by travelling to distant places of the country and meeting them. She would sometimes reach out to the people, acknowledge their greetings and often throw garlands to the public, in a style reminiscent of her mother-in-law Indira. She has remained something of an enigma for a vast section of the people.

As a responsible politician Sonia always remains in touch with her constituency, Rae Bareli. After being elected as MP, she has visited the constituency several times and toured many blocks, listened to people's problems and solved them. Better roads and improvement in power supply are some of the results of her initiatives.

Some of the milestones in the development of the constituency by the Congress are Indian Telephone Industries (ITI), National Thermal Power Corporation (NTPC) and Indira Gandhi Rashtriya Udyan Academy (IGRUA). Sonia's name has become synonymous with development in the constituency. The ITI was on the verge of closure. Six thousand employees were fighting for survival. Within a year, Sonia handed out Rs. 500 crore grant for the ITI's revival. Link roads and bridges got a facelift after she got Rs. 200 crore sanctioned from the Centre's road fund and Rs. 132 crore bonanza came next, under Rajiv Gandhi Rural Electrification Programme. The Union Power Minister sanctioned Rs. 29.13 crore to revamp and augment power capacity.

Sonia has humane touch also. She made rounds of hospitals when Rae Bareli was hit by the JE (Japanese Encephalitis) epidemic in 2005. She later equipped the hospital with ventilators and Elisa readers and also announced setting up of a trauma centre there.

PEOPLE'S POLITICIAN

Sonia's humility, sympathy, kindness and tolerance are great qualities, which endeared her to one and all. Position and honour don't make her a different person. By her unique affability, honest image and knack for providing good governance she has become people's politician. She has won the hearts of the crores of people who are aware of her rational thinking and approach. That is why wherever she goes, people—young and old, men and women—gather around her in large numbers. They somehow want to have a glimpse of her. It is generally noticed that people climb on walls, trees and electric poles or whatever else that serve the purpose, to have a look at her.

As party President Sonia travels to different parts of the country quite often not only to do rallies but also to be with the people in the time of their crisis. It is the attraction that people come in large number to listen to her. Attraction is so high that no barrier is strong enough to debar people from attending her meetings. She is a star attraction of sorts. People feel delighted when they see her.

Sonia visited Ahmedabad in 2002 to participate in the Sadhbhavna Rally. People gathered there from all-around. It was time for her to show off women power. The male leaders in the Congress, like Kamal Nath, Ahmed Patel and Amarsinh Chaudhary, deliberately took a back seat and watched the women at work. In fact, they joined the 2.5 km long procession only at Bhadra where Sonia climbed onto an open jeep and waved at the enthusiastic crowds. Some 10,000 people participated in the rally, many of them came just to see Sonia, proving the rally several shades popular.

The show at Porebander, where Sonia addressed a rally was much bigger with nearly 50,000 people turned up to hear her call to combat the communalism. She accused the BJP for allowing the violence to persist for long with a view to popularise the vote for the next assembly elections.

Women had come from Rajasthan, Madhya Pradesh, Maharashtra and several parts of Gujarat and even West Bengal to express solidarity with her. Some of the banners stood out for the direct assault on the NDA Government saying, "*Zalim ko jo na toke, woh shamil hai zulm main; Katil ko jo na roke, who katil ke saath hai.*"

To arouse nationalistic spirit, the Congress party decided to re-enact the Dandi March on the occasion of its 75th anniversary in 2005. The Dandi March took place in 1930 when Mahatma Gandhi broke salt law by picking up a handful of salt. The March was first enacted in 1988. Rajiv then flagged off the *Yatra*. Sonia also participated in it.

The objective of the re-enactment of the March by the party under Sonia was to recapture the spirit as also to reaffirm commitment to the welfare and well-being of the people with a resolve to protect and promote Gandhian values, especially those relating to social harmony and justice. Elaborating the party's intention the Congress President said,

"We may believe in Gandhi and his thoughts, but the bigger message would be when new generation gets inspired by his principles and ideals and understands that the path taken by Bapu was the most sublime."

There was great zeal and enthusiasm among the people for the March. Sonia administered the pledge to the participants, which included CWC members, Union Ministers, AICC office-bearers, MPs, MLAs, leaders and workers. She led the *padayatra* from the Sabarmati Ashram with the followers. The response of the people in towns and villages along the *yatra* route was overwhelming. Thousands of people lined up on both sides of the roads to greet the participants with love, affection and hospitality. During the halts, the leaders participated in many constructive activities like cleanliness campaign, educating villagers on hygiene and sanitation and exchanging information on economic activities. The *yatra* ended at coastal village Dandi.

Governance

6

VISION FOR INDIA

Elections are important in a democratic process. Equally important is the party's goal and vision. This is the first time that the Congress party under Sonia is leading a coalition government at the Centre. By dint of her position she has a major say in the government and each policy adopted by it certainly have her approval. It is her foresight that will reflect in the long run.

Sonia also has a vision and that is strong, united, secular and modern India, an India in which poverty is eradicated and all forms of exploitations—social, economic and political—are ended. She has her own dream—the dream that her husband cherished for the 21st century. She doesn't just dream but a real achiever. The result is discernable, as the UPA Government has made large public investments in critical areas.

Sonia has the progressive and visionary approach and wants to see India as a developed and prosperous country with no exploitation of the poor or harassment of the innocent people. Her main concerns are welfare of the people and impetus to the growth. She understands that the barometer of progress lies with the improvement of the condition of the *aam admi*.

Sonia wants to see a corruption-free administration. She also wants universal implementation and proper distribution of all welfare schemes that are meant for the deprived sections of the society. In this country corruption is the main reason behind the poor implementation of centrally sponsored schemes in states. That is why she has called upon the bureaucrats to show sincerity in implementing the projects under the timeframe.

UPA'S COMMAND AND CONTROL

The post of UPA Chairperson entails responsibility and Sonia gives quite a creditable account of herself as she has been discharging that task with utmost foresight and competence so that the Government runs smoothly. She possesses all the qualities that go to the making of a capable leader/ mentor. She took command at a time when both Indian polity and economy were in transition. The polity was changing to a coalition government while the economy was adjusting to globalisation. There was a need to take a balanced view of the both and she has been doing that adroitly in concert with the masters of economics—Prime Minister, Finance Minister and Planning Commission Deputy Chairman—for the crucial job. People of the country are looking at her for effective governance. As she has clear perspective on economic policies it became easy for her to design plans and programmes to be achieved.

Sonia takes the role of governance seriously. As heading a coalition, to keep it intact is a great challenge for her. Not only she has to ensure smooth functioning of the Government but also makes sure that the Government works for the progress of the country and betterment of its people. She has to prove that her brand of governance is totally different from what the people have experienced so far.

As Sonia functions as a pivot of the UPA Government she has been able to give impetus to the rural development through scores of schemes in operation for the benefit of the *aam admi*. She has called upon Congress Chief Ministers and party leaders to deliver the promises made to the people and address issues concerning the weaker sections.

The country is ridden with various forms of corruption, poverty and crime. There is a need for a dynamic leadership who can transform India to a land of peace and prosperity and Sonia has bravely come forward to lead the country in achieving that goal. She is with the task almost as impossible as climbing the Mt Everest but doing her best for that.

The UPA chief is committed to provide a corruption-free, transparent and accountable government and towards that goal she has unleashed the creative energies of those who are skilful in their respective fields. The UPA Government has already delivered substantially on its commitments. Never before had a Government fulfilled so many of its stated commitments so soon after coming to power.

As UPA Chairperson, Sonia ensures that the Government make effort to improve the conditions of the people as envisioned in the party manifesto. She is deeply concerned about the weaker sections, particularly women, Dalits and minorities. The Government under her supervision has come up with several excellent economic policies and raising itself to meet the serious challenges facing the country besides protecting its unity and integrity.

Sonia was an avid opponent of obnoxious legislation POTA. She questioned it when the legislation was passed on the strength of a technical majority by making both the Houses of Parliament sit together. As for her commitment to implement Congress manifesto, the UPA Government took up on a priority basis to scrap the POTA. The Government constituted POTA review committee and with its recommendation released persons wrongfully hauled up under the law in Gujarat. After POTA, the Government took another major step to undo damages caused to history books by the previous dispensation. The Congress party always criticised previous government for its proposition to damage the history of freedom struggle. The Government has now corrected them. Steps were taken to reverse trend of communalisation of education. Under these, a panel of historians reviewed the text of history books of National Council of Educational Research and Training (NCERT) and Government implemented its recommendations. Besides, all autonomous bodies under the Ministry of Human Resources Development were requested to undertake a review of other activities that possibly gave rise to the perception of communalisation of education and take suitable corrective measures. A revised national curriculum framework for school education is in place. The Central Advisory Board on Education (CABE) has been revised to facilitate wider consultation.

The UPA headed by Sonia came into being aimed at providing a responsible, responsive, caring and inclusive government. The UPA constituents also pledged to preserve, protect and promote social harmony and to enforce the law without fear or favour to deal with all fundamentalist elements that try to disturb social harmony and peace. The constituents are committed to ensure that the economy grows at faster pace in a sustained manner over a decade or more and in a manner that generates employment so that each family is assured a viable livelihood.

The Congress-led UPA Government has set a 10 per cent growth target during the 11th Plan. The party's resolution at the plenary in Hyderabad indicated that the policies being pursued by the Government are such that they benefit the *aam admi*.

After coming to power the UPA Government is able to give a new momentum to the economy. The party is of the view that the entrepreneurs, scientists and professionals need liberation from the shackles of controls as well as creation of dynamic environment to utilise their contribution for the growth of the country. On the issue of FDI in retail sector, the party wants that the supply chain for the retailers have to be strengthened.

Sonia remains concerned at the impact of price rise on the people and directed the Government to keep a close watch on it. Thinking that price rise would put extra burden on the people, she urged the Government to reconsider its decision to hike prices of rice and wheat for the public distribution system (PDS) for those living below the poverty line (BPL). She also directed the Government to monitor availability of food grains and other essential commodities of daily use such as kerosene, cooking gas etc. so that people don't suffer from its scarcity. About the PDS, the Congress party maintains that the subsidy shouldn't be cut down for the BPL families and the level of quantity of food grains supplied to them be maintained.

The Congress President expressed satisfaction that the agriculture has got a new thrust after the UPA came to power and called upon the Ministry to keep the trend up by pushing recommendations of the National Commission of Farmers (NCF). The NCF gives suggestions to the Government from time to time regarding policy matters.

Sonia is closely associated with the government in policy formulation, monitoring and implementation. The party workers are kept informed at every stage about the changes that take place. They have the impression that once the party is in power, they are neglected. The Congress chief believes that only political mobilisation would give them a sense of involvement and participation and enthuse them to work for much wider social mobilisation. It is necessary for the success of development programmes and for sustaining popular support for the party. Party's objective is empowerment of the people. This can only take place when people are made aware of their rights and collectively demand them.

Sonia exercises great policy influence and remains instrumental pertaining to all issues and affairs. There are two reasons for this: First, being the Congress President she sought electoral mandate to run the government, though she never projected herself as a prime ministerial candidate and second, the Congress is a responsible political party; country's overall development is its prime concern. Any deviation from the set path can be awful for the party.

The task is rather difficult because she is heading a coalition government and some parties are supporting the government from outside. Moreover, to go by the coalition principles, she has to take care of their demands. Albeit! she sincerely tries to tackle such problems in a best possible way.

Further, this is the first time that two different persons are heading the party and the government. Under such circumstances perfect coordination between them and between party and government are required. The onus is more on Sonia because it is she whom the people have given the mandate.

As Chairperson of the UPA, Sonia along with Prime Minister released the National Common Minimum Programme (NCMP). It covers various sectors where the Government wants to give top priority. The prominent sectors are employment, agriculture, education/health, women/children, SC/ST, social harmony, defence, foreign policy etc.

Employment is a major problem in our country. The NCMP pledges an Act to ensure 100 days of employment on public works programme. As per the NCMP, the agriculture has to be given more attention to boost production. For this, the irrigation sector needed investment priority. The rural cooperative credit system has been nursed back to health.

To improve upon education and health, the Government has decided to rise public spending to 6 per cent of GDP. Mid-day meal programmes in primary and secondary schools has been intensified.

The NCMP also talks about reservation in the private sector and for this dialogue with political parties, industry and organisations has been initiated. The NCMP clearly underlines the need for 33 per cent reservation for women in Assemblies and Lok Sabha. To remove evil practices of child labour it stresses on taking effective measures. Communal riots bring about heavy loss of lives and cause damage to property besides tarnishing of country's image internationally. To deal with such violence a model law has been enacted and states are encouraged to adopt it.

On foreign policy, the Government has decided to pursue an independent foreign policy keeping in mind the past traditions. Dialogues with neighbouring Pakistan are taking place regularly on tricky issues besides pursuing CBMs (confidence building measures) to enhance mutual understanding. The NCMP also calls for maintaining a credible nuclear weapon programme. The Government has also entered into a civilian nuclear deal with the US.

It is an uphill task for Sonia to implement Congress manifesto as well as the NCMP. To keep both the pledges, she needs to be very pragmatic. Besides, there remain pulls and pressures from the coalition partners for this and that and she sometimes gives in unwillingly to accommodate their wishes.

The UPA with Sonia at the helm is committed to enhance the welfare of the poor and well-being of the farmers, farm labourers and workers, particularly those in the unorganised sector and assure a secured future for their families in every respect. The UPA wants to empower women politically, educationally, economically and legally to provide full equality of opportunity, particularly in education and employment for scheduled castes, scheduled tribes, other backward classes and minorities.

On the economic front the Government has been working out plans and programmes to make the country an economic superpower and consolidate the reform process. The Government commitment is to protect the poor and the disadvantaged groups.

Sonia wants to see Indian economy strong, viable and people-oriented. For this she felt the need for changes both in policies and programmes. Most of these issues had clearly been identified in the election manifesto of the party. The Congress-ruled states go by that set policies. They not only implement the Congress promises made to the people but also set examples for good governance.

Besides programmes for the benefit of farmers and industry the Congress party also wants to strengthen the Panchayati Raj system and make its functioning flawless. From attaining of Independence till today, the party gave attention to the development of the country and to serve its people. This had been the tradition of Nehru, Indira and Rajiv governments. Sonia too has pledged to follow that path. For her, politics is an opportunity to serve the people.

The Congress party is committed to revive the country's economy and to provide basic amenities to the poorest of the poor. It believes in the empowerment of the Indian women so that they can find their rightful place as equal partner in every sphere. The party makes all-out efforts to provide the new generation an opportunity so that they can become fit to meet challenges in the 21st century.

The Congress President considers that poverty and unemployment were the two major problems being faced by the people. The UPA Government has taken several measures to improve the situation and lead the nation into the future of prosperity and happiness. "The party is aware of the basic needs of different neglected sections like weavers, fishermen, rural artisans and farmers and has formulated policies for their uplift. The party strongly believes in the concept of Panchayati Raj system that is why it gives thrust to it. Rajiv had canalised the flow of funds directly to the Village Panchayats for implementation of developmental programmes," she said.

Sonia ensures that the UPA Government implement the party's manifesto in letter and spirit as these programmes have vision and ideology. She has denied that the programmes launched by the Government had technocratic or bureaucratic intervention and cautions the Congress leaders holding office at different levels against ignoring the party organisation.

The UPA Government shall be best remembered for its people-oriented policies. These policies would go a long way in transforming conditions of the common people as well as of rural infrastructure. Brief reviews of the programmes that have been launched through the patronage of UPA Chairperson are as under:

Rural development: National Rural Development Act is in effect. For the first time it recognises the right to work as a fundamental legal right and entitles the rural poor to guaranteed employment. Through the Act, Sonia takes the *aam admi* towards progress and happiness, not misery and ruin. The above law is its instance because it was her brainchild. She first conceived its framework way back in 2002. Billed as a key Government programme initiated in tune with the NCMP, the move has bolstered Congress party's *aam admi* image. The ambitious law has constitutional safeguard, i.e., right to employment for at least 100 days of work in a year for household members of the country, to provide economic and social security to the poor and unemployed rural people. The employment guarantee scheme is an example of fulfilment of the promises made by the Congress party for the rural people in its manifesto. The scheme caters to 72 crore rural people. Initially 200 backward districts have been covered. The minimum wage is worked out as per the Minimum Wage Act, 1948. The wage paid is Rs. 60 and the women are given priority. Panchayats have been given responsibility to finalise and approve the projects and also monitor them. The application for work has to be made to the local Panchayat which would verify whether the applicant resides in its area and is an adult. If identity is authenticated then the Panchayat registers the applicant. A job card is issued to the applicant household. After the card is issued, the registered household can apply for work.

Bharat Nirman: To enable the economic reform programme in order to balance the growth imperative with a view to bridge the urban-rural divide, the UPA Government felt the need to build rural infrastructure. With this objective it launched the Rs. 1,74,000 crore Bharat Nirman programme in less than two years in office. No government launched such a massive programme on rural development in such a short time. It is a six-pronged four-year time-bound programme. The identified goals to be achieved are irrigation, rural water supply, rural housing, rural road, rural telephone and rural electrification. In four of these areas universal coverage would be ensured. Under it every village having a population of over a thousand would have an all-weather road, every habitation would have water supply and a telephone and all the villages would be electrified. Housing shortage is a serious problem. Under the programme, about 60 lakh houses to be built to address rural homelessness and 10 million hectares of land to be brought under irrigation capacity.

Women empowerment: Sonia wants real empowerment and uplift of the women for she believes that the progress for a few is not a real progress of the nation. She is aware of the difficulties that they face in everyday life. To protect the interest of the women the UPA Government enacted a law that shields them from domestic violence in the family and sexual exploitation at the work places. Several other steps have been taken to put women's foot on a solid base. Through the enactment of Protection of Women from Domestic Violence Act, an effective protection has been provided to women who became victims of violence of any kind occurring within a family. The Act enables women to negotiate non-abusive and non-violent matrimonial or other domestic relationships and provide them a civil remedy hitherto not available in the criminal law regime. The Hindu Succession Act has been amended to make women's inheritance rights in parents' property equal to men's across states, overriding any inconsistent state laws. The Parliament has also passed a bill for effecting changes in the criminal procedure code, which provides safeguards for women in terms of bar on arrest at night. The Government has enacted laws and legislation for the protection of the women and children. Through a bill the Factories Act, 1948 has been amended to provide flexibility in working hours of women while providing a suitable safeguard to ensure their well-being. This would help employment in the services sector, especially software services and data centres. Another bill seeks amendment to the Prevention of Child Marriage Act. The Government also proposed to amend the Immoral Traffic Prevention Act, 1956 in order to make the provisions of law more stringent for traffickers, pimps and brothel owners, and to omit such provisions of the Act as those are discriminatory towards women who are victims of commercial and sexual exploitation. In India women comprise half of the country's population but equal opportunity for development and social prestige for them remain a distant dream. The Congress President felt the need to change such attitudes and enact new law to make gender equality possible and called for a national initiative, involving political parties, voluntary organisations, NGOs and media to prevent all forms of atrocities against women. The initiatives included focusing of welfare of workers in the unorganised sector and taking measures to end scavenging.

She is totally committed to the welfare of the women. Concerned over the status of the women, she stressed that there must be reservation for women in national and state legislatures, like the Panchayats, and hopes that some way would be found on the question of earmarking one-third reservation for women in elected legislatures. A bill with one-third reservation for women in legislature remains a top priority of the Congress President. Sonia has always been making strong pitch for the bill. She truly stands behind the bill and holds out hope that some way would be found. Her efforts are on for building a consensus on this and also lobbying support for new proposals that include increase in the number of seats by one-third of the present strength to accommodate women. On the part of the Government it held meeting with all UPA constituents and all Opposition parties. Discussions have been held with women group and other stakeholders. The Government argument is that the number of seats in Parliament and state legislatures should be increased to reflect the population growth. Although the BJP, the second largest political party, has promised to support any consensus among the parties, some differences have appeared among the others. To break logjam the BJP, however, says that the EC recommendation should be adopted.

Minority welfare: Sonia always strives for promotion of communal harmony and wants rational development of all sections of the society. About welfare of minorities, she believes that though Muslims enjoy equal rights under the Constitution, there is a gap between rights in law and their realisation. She considers the development level of Muslim population in terms of equality and social justice is quite low and underlines the need to reduce level of deprivation that prevails with the weakest and the most deprived. The community is underrepresented in public employment and public life. So the task should be to generate awareness of the problems that exist and explore equitable and cooperative solution. For this she called for affirmative action to increase Muslim representations in public employment and access to educational institutions. On the need for special educational schemes for minority community the UPA Government set up National Commission of Minorities for Education and Employment, besides other programme for their uplift. National Commission for Minority Educational Institutions (NCMEI) was established through an Act. The Act has also been widened through a bill. It would ensure that the provisions of the Constitution giving the minorities the right to establish and administer educational institutions of their choice be implemented effectively. A commission was set up to identify how best the welfare of socially and economically backward sections among the minority, including through reservations in education and Government, may be ensured. A committee studied in-depth the condition of the minorities and recommended steps for their economic and social development and empowerment. The promotion of Urdu language is another step that the Government has taken. As per the plan the Government would open Urdu medium schools in districts where Muslim population is more than 10 per cent. To improve education standards of the community specific schemes would be brought in the 11th five-year plan. Backward Muslims to be given some reservation under 12 per cent reservation mooted for OBCs in elite educational institutions of the Government.

Education: As both Congress manifesto and NCMP talk about improvement of elementary education, Sonia makes sure that the UPA Government does something in that direction. As a result an Education Cess at the rate of two per cent is in place to raise resources for providing universal elementary education. A non-lapsable fund called Prarambhik Shiksha Kosh has been set up to receive the proceeds to finance the elementary education, Sarva Shiksha Abhiyan (SSA) and the mid-day meal scheme. New elementary schools have been opened in various localities/villages all over the country under the SSA. The SSA seeks to bridge all gender and social category gaps at primary stage by 2007 and at elementary education level by 2010.

Health: Poor healthcare facilities in rural areas are cause of concern. To improve it the UPA Government launched the National Rural Health Mission (NRHM). Under it Accredited

Social Health Activists (ASHAs) have been appointed in all villages in 10 high-focus states. Integrated Child Development Service (ICDS) schemes are aimed at holistic development of children and pregnant/lactating mothers of disadvantaged sections, by providing services through Anganwadi Centre such as supplementary nutrition, immunisation, health check-up, referral services, pre-school and non-formal education. Government has sanctioned 467 additional ICDS projects and 1,88 lakh Anganwadi Centres in order to ensure one centre in every habitation, as per the existing population of 1,000 (700 for tribal/hilly/desert areas).

Besides the above people-oriented policies, the UPA Government is able to boost rural economy and in combating poverty to a great extent. The NREGS is getting tremendous response and has provided jobs to crores of rural people. Several other programmes of the Government have been put in place in pursuance of its agenda to build infrastructure and to ameliorate the conditions of the weaker sections, particularly women. The Government is committed to be with the *aam admi* through job-oriented growth of the economy.

The UPA Government has plans to provide justice to the *aam admi* by setting up Gram Nyayalaya (village court) in rural areas. To make it more viable, Sonia-led National Advisory Council (NAC) put forward some suggestions so that the process doesn't become cumbersome, dilatory and expensive. The Government plan is that the Nyayalayas be set up in the Tehsil headquarters but she wants it to be as close to the people as possible. Though the court fee would be very low, the NAC has made some changes in the provision so that the high courts can raise the fee amount at a later stage without amending the law.

The other issue on the NAC agenda is to remove regional disparities in economic growth. On this the NAC took note of the analysis of the causes underlying the gap between rich and poor in states and the problems faced by the less developed states. Several measures have been taken to promote growth, infrastructure and human development on a more equal and rational basis.

Sonia is for stronger cooperation between the Government and the civil society to make better India. This was understood while delivering a keynote address at the Hindustan Times Leadership Summit on the theme 'Building A Better Future'. She said the corporate sector was ready to carry forward that goal and called upon the Government to create an institutional framework to involve civil-society organisations in the democratic and developmental process to canalise their inputs so that all Indians have a better future. She was optimistic about it saying better future could be built through vibrant partnership between government and the civil society and felt that the NGOs and other voluntary agencies and community associations have made their mark in fields like education, health and rural development.

Sonia considers the coalition government as a 'national imperative' to fight the BJP's politics of hate. She at the same time also feels the need for a parallel effort to rebuild the organisation and help it serve as a bridge between the government and the people. Her idea is to help regain its status as an organisation of social forces. Taking note of the prevailing ground realities she feels that it is necessary for renewed collaboration and cooperation to fight the forces of communalism.

The Congress President wishes that the Government accomplish Rajiv's unfinished tasks. This means, empowering the people at the lowest level with a modern and tech-savvy approach. With this goal the UPA Government has set up Information Technology Commission headed by Sam Pitroda, the man whom Rajiv made Scientific Adviser.

Pitroda stepped on India's telecom scene about two decades ago. At that time there were 20 lakh landlines for approximately 75 crore people. Phones were not efficient and there was hardly any access to global community. Today, there are over 8 crore phones—5 crore landlines and 3 crore mobiles. He is now thinking of next telecom revolution to keep rural India reasonably well connected. It is felt that with the onset of telecom regulation there would be greater transparency and lesser corruption in the country.

Sonia ensures greater coordination between the party and the Government. She feels that the party keep an eye on the functioning of the Government. The party's motto is service to develop the nation that is why she always advises her party leaders to follow the manifesto tooth and nail. She thinks the party has the obligation to work for the welfare of the nation.

Sonia wants her party leaders develop such sense of values and ethics that would strengthen their character. She also wants practice of austerity and simplicity in public life and never gives credence to misuse of position. She is a brand that encourages the spirit of service and sacrifice in politics. "Practise what you preach" is her motto. This was evident when she told partymen to follow this creed at the one day AICC session in August 2004 held to commemorate Rajiv's birth anniversary.

Sonia never tolerates wrongdoing. On knowing that some MLAs of Uttaranchal were enjoying the privilege of a minister, she showed her disapproval of it and took steps to put an end to the practice of according ministerial ranks. The Chief Minister of the state granted ministerial ranks to around 200 people. They enjoyed all the privileges of a minister—official car, security and telephone facilities. She took exception to the practice of providing ranks of cabinet and ministers to chairpersons of corporations, boards and councils and called for an end to such unwarranted expenditure.

Sonia believes that central as well as state governments owe it to the people to provide an administration that is known for probity and austerity. Institutions formed for ensuring probity in public life should be further empowered to discharge their functions and obligations properly, without discriminating political affiliations.

In a letter to the party's chief ministers she stressed that government, ministers and leaders maintain austerity and follow code of ethics. In a sharp reminder that they are the servants of the people and not their masters, she issued directives to party bosses—both state ministers and organisational bigwigs—to cut ostentation and refrain from ugly display of power.

This is not the first time that Sonia has told her flocks to stay simple. Many times she expressed dislike to such ostentation but her word had not the requisite impact. She again sent an 18-point dos and don'ts. In her letter, she said, "It is shocking to see that violations of codes are being done even by Congress-ruled states." Her fresh directive had five specific points for PCCs and 13 for state governments, some of them sweeping in nature, which forced ministers to take a crash course in asceticism.

The code lays down strict measures like only economy-class air travel for ministers and government officials, putting the cap on official telephone bill of ministers and officials, cutting STD and ISD facilities on official phones and specifying that red lights and sirens can be used only on vehicles of the governors and chief ministers.

Aimed at curbing misuse of government money and impolite display of power, the code says that the ministers should have only one official vehicle. The foundation stone-laying ceremony should be discouraged; celebration of new years and religious festivals at government expense should be stopped and state aeroplanes and helicopters should be used sparingly. She even frowned on invitation cards for dinners and luncheons being printed at government expenses.

Sonia always tries to nurture people-party-government relations and strengthen the organisation and its social base and is determined to continue party's battle against the communal ideology of the Sangh Parivar. She stands by the core issues of maintaining peace and harmony in the country and allows no polarisation on the basis of region, religion or caste.

There is greater interaction between governments and party organisations towards finding a solution. There is also involvement of the party in the information, implementation and monitoring of developmental programmes. Elections are won on achievements that are visible. Sonia has urged the chief ministers to be sensitive to the problems of the weaker sections of the society. They have been asked to be sensitive to different perspective of the people and measures taken in time so that they don't reject the party later. She even directed the Maharashtra Chief Minister to go out among the people to express solidarity with them when the state was in the grip of crisis perpetrated by torrential rains and high tides.

Sonia has urged all Congressmen to guard against factionalism and infighting and suggested that they solve their differences harmoniously and amicably. They are asked to approach the Government with people's problems, not for own benefits. She advised partymen to learn to live for others. She also reminded them about the lofty ideals and principles such as unity, discipline, service and dedication, which are the inherent principles of the party. She even reiterated some moral code for the partymen, such as to stick to ideology, lead a simple life and shun pompous display of wealth. She called upon them to follow in the footsteps of our fathers and freedom fighters, go by the code of conduct, project acceptable face in public, fight against social evils, fulfil party's commitments to *aam admi*, cultivate traits like honesty and determination. Some points that she doesn't want to follow by the partymen are: No lavish wedding and birthdays, no use of muscle powers and steer clear of partisan politics.

Sonia has urged the Ministers and leaders to be more accessible to grass-root party workers and address their grievances. She wants that Central ministers hold meetings with workers while touring different parts of the country. By doing thus they would be able to know their views regarding the Government and the party.

The 18-point austerity measure that she directed her chief ministers to follow was a fitting rejoinder for the Opposition, which always doubted Sonia's competence. By her sheer ability she has now proved the Opposition wrong for doubting her comprehension and understanding. Becoming fully convinced of what she said, former Prime Minister Chandrasekhar appreciated her line of thinking.

Sonia has requested the political parties to play a pro-active role in monitoring and mobilisation of the programmes.

Terming the rural job guarantee legislation as 'truly radical', she cautioned saying, "the real changes has begun in making sure that the legislation works in the manner it is meant to, in a manner that will tangibly impact the lives of crores of our brothers and sisters in rural India." She is also against unnecessary administrative delay in clearing and implementing the welfare measures.

Sonia is a person of uprightness and plays clean politics, come what may. She loathes persons who misuse power and authority and never dither to take stern action against them. She is proud of the family she belongs to and defends unflinchingly any attempt to defame it. She is also very particular about maintaining dignity of the family and the party. Any attempt to malign such precepts is against propriety and she takes umbrage to anybody who tries to defame it.

Sonia convened the Chandigarh conclave with the purpose of influencing the course of political atmosphere and policies of its government in states. She took the manifesto commitment seriously and remained firm that pledges have to be fulfilled. All leaders, central and state, are equally responsible to work on the promises made to the people. She wants that the progress reports of the governments be shared with the public every two months.

The Congress-led UPA Government has embarked on an ambitious social security package for workers in the unorganised sector. The party has mobilised cadres, including that of the frontal organisations in a big way to explain to people what these packages are for. They are to network with action groups or community-based organisations for social audit and monitoring. The Right to Information (RTI) Act has come into effect. People can use it to demand transparency and accountability in implementation of the programmes.

The programmes that the Congress party has launched are not a result of just technocratic or bureaucratic interventions. They are the programmes of the party, borne out of its political vision and ideology. The Government and other agencies at the Centre and the states are responsible for their implementation. Sonia has asked the party organisation to own these programmes and play pivotal role in their implementation. She also feels it necessary to make the people known what the unique contribution the Congress party is making. There is a need to make them aware that the NCMP mostly reflects the Congress' own manifesto. The achievements of the NCMP are, therefore, the fulfilment of the party's objectives.

The suffering of people from disasters upsets Sonia very much. Every year natural calamities happen in many states. To give immediate succour to the people, the UPA Government has constituted National Disaster Management Authority. Although the Centre moves ahead with its plan, the primary responsibility for disaster management in all aspects would obviously remain with that of the head of the government, which shall review the preparedness for different types of natural disasters from time to time.

The odds relating to administrative shortcomings pinch all. Keeping this in mind, the UPA Government has set up Administrative Reforms Commission. The RTI Act is another step in this direction that provides opportunity to the common people to seek information from the Government. It empowers the people to fight against corruption by directly seeking information on developments.

Sonia wants efficient public service and delivery system especially for the less privileged section of the society. She believes that the basic responsibility for delivering on social basics lies with the states and for this has called upon the Government to ensure that the Scheduled Caste and Scheduled Tribe students get their scholarship on the first day of every month, the retired citizens get pension and provident fund payments on time and a citizen get passport easily. The maternity benefits being provided to needy women under a scheme get these before the maternity period is over. She said that if irregularities are noticed in the delivery system, they should be removed without much delay.

Sonia has found some of the Government rules and procedures part of the problem and feels the need to refurbish the administrative system so that it facilitates the *aam admi* in their dealings with the administration. In her view, the economic reforms shouldn't signify abdication of the role of the Government. They signify for making the Government at all levels caring, particularly in power and waterfront, function better and in a more consumer-friendly manner.

Sonia is of the view that liberalisation shouldn't suggest any erosion in the assertive role of the Government and reforms must consider for improving the functioning of public institutions, particularly in education and health. All these require investment and changes in structure and procedure. The administration makes effort to apply the law of the land, without fear or favour, against all those who disturb social peace.

It has been found that the procurement through public contracts is not transparent. The stranglehold of contractors and middlemen in development programmes often has nexus with both bureaucrats and politicians. This tendency has to do away with so that injustice on the people, particularly on the poor and the deprived, is stopped.

The UPA Government has increased budgetary outlays in areas like education, agricultural research, health and nutrition. The mid-day meal has been strengthened by the provision of cooked meals and scaling up the level of assistance. The mid-day meals are now being provided even during the vacations in drought-affected areas.

The Government has launched major programmes like rural infrastructure and health. The Bharat Nirman programme is perhaps the most comprehensive and expensive rural infrastructure programme in the country. The Government is looking into the details of urban renewal mission that covers scores of cities in the country. Sonia has asked the Congress-ruled states to take maximum advantage of this programme.

However, the Government is facing challenges in reversing the declining agricultural growth rate that was due to unfavourable natural condition. Unless this is done, it will be impossible to take care the well-being of the millions of rural poor, or support efforts in infrastructure, industry and services. For this the states have to improve their fiscal positions. As far as Congress-ruled states are concerned, they should take a lead in this regard.

The UPA Government under Sonia takes care of the farming community. The Government is very much aware of the credit needs of the small and marginal farmers and have decided to reform the rural cooperative structure. The chief ministers have been directed to discuss any problem with the Prime Minister at the National Development Council.

Congress party is committed to welfare of the weaker sections of the society. With this aim the party has resurrected the Garibi Hatao programme that was first coined by Indira in 1970s. Under it the UPA Government has adopted a 20-point programme (TPP), initially adopted by Indira in 1975, with a view to eradicate poverty and meet the challenges of the 21st century. The Government considers that the TPP would reflect is objectives about the anti-poverty measures. The TPP is a mix of social sector schemes whose implementation is to be closely monitored so that the benefits reach the targeted sections. For this purpose four monitoring mechanism will be set up from the block to central levels. It will come into force from new financial year. The TPP covers poverty eradication, food security, welfare measures for labour, SC/ST/OBCs and minorities, farmer support, education, health and housing for all, power to people, provision of drinking water, development of backward areas and rural roads and e-governance etc. Altogether it has 64 items.

Sonia has found administrative shortcomings in the delivery system and wants the Government bring a change in it. Expressing concern about it she said, "Our programmes do not always work the way they are planned. Delivery system claims too large a share of the outlets. The benefits always do not reach the poor." Steps are on to improve the delivery system and to bring about a radical change in implementation of developmental schemes. While expressing immense confidence that the scheme would change the face of rural India, UPA Chairperson, however, warned against the *sab chalta hai* attitude.

The Congress is singularly credited for the empowerment of the Panchayats and Nagar Palikas and that is one big innovation in the delivery system. The party has succeeded in the political revival and now the administrative and fiscal strengthening is being looked into. Law and order is another aspect that influences growth and development of a country. If atmosphere is peaceful the country can advance through path of progress otherwise the reverse happens.

Naxalite, Maoist and ULFA violence in some parts of the country is cause of great concern and the UPA Government has taken tough stand to contain these. The Government is making efforts to improve the functioning of the police and security forces. The channels for dialogue have been kept open so that understanding could be reached and wanton killings of innocent men, women and children stopped.

The issue of land and land rights has achieved greater dimension in Andhra Pradesh. The central and state governments are looking for some ways to come to a solution. The Congress President wants a time-bound campaign for resolving all land-related disputes and updating land records. The disturbances caused by insurgents in the country have retarded progress of programmes pertaining to rural development.

The Centre is making efforts to find a solution to the Kashmir issue and held several round of peace talks. The Government's peace process received a fillip when Sonia assured the moderate Hurriyat Conference leaders that the Government is committed to find a solution to it and told them that the gun culture and violence should have no place in the state.

To put forward the peace process the Centre invited the separatists to participate in the roundtable conferences held at New Delhi and Srinagar but some of them didn't join the negotiating table. Seeing their keenness low Sonia urged the separatist leaders to participate in the roundtable and other democratic processes arguing unless they come forward how can there be a solution. She said, "Dialogue is the only process that can solve all issues and the Centre is trying to bring the people out of the bloodshed. The representatives should take part in the conferences convened by the Centre and put forward their views." According to her, peace process and confidence-building measures were essential as those would help in the growth of trade and tourism possibilities.

India has been fighting terrorism for several years. Sonia has stressed upon tackling terrorism firmly and without any compromise. Addressing a CPP meeting she urged the UPA Government and party leaders to ensure that no community should feel it is under siege or target of suspicion. About complaints that Muslim community was being allegedly targeted and subjected to 'witch-hunt' after the Mumbai serial blasts, she told the Government that steps must be taken to check any such apprehension. She made it clear that there could be 'no compromise' in combating terrorism in all its manifestations and maintained that India's secular ethos must be nurtured and enriched. "Secularism has bound our country for centuries. It has been our strength, our defining characteristic. We must never ever forget that if communal harmony is disturbed our very future is in peril. Those who wish to weaken and damage our country will always seek to divide and polarise our society. Under no circumstances should we allow this to happen," she said and emphasised that anti-social and anti-national elements be clearly identified and dealt with firmly. She, however, suggested for fully equipped, properly trained and highly motivated anti-terrorism force in each state to fight the menace of terrorism.

Sonia is steadfast in its commitment to coalition politics but warned the alliance partners not to cross the limit of constructive criticism. The party cautioned the partners against rocking the coalition boat too hard and reminded that the alternative was too dangerous to even contemplate. The political resolution adopted at the party's plenary session gave vent to the coalition leaders' continuing fire-fighting. The party made it clear to the Left parties that it could not be at the receiving end of their pressure tactics at frequent intervals.

Despite odds Sonia's resolve to make the coalition a success has shown results. Whenever any coalition partner is dissatisfied with the Government's stand, she intervenes and makes them understand reasons. Several times she met Left leaders and sorted out differences. The UPA Chairperson and the Prime Minister allayed the Left leaders' apprehensions through talks and sometimes by debate in Parliament. The Left's dissatisfaction over Government's disinvestments plan of the public sector undertakings (PSUs), employees provident fund (EPF) rate, airport privatisation and foreign direct investment (FDI) in retail were assuaged. Both of them assured the Left leaders that the Government would do whatever best for the country.

As leader of the responsible political party, Sonia herself has vision for the country. As there are certain compulsions of coalition politics she refrained from resisting the Government's line on disinvestments of the country's one of the largest public sector undertaking Bharat Heavy Electricals Limited (BHEL). At a meeting with Left leaders Sonia heard their interpretation of passages relating to Navratna PSUs in the NCMP. The only point she raised was about mobilisation of resources for the employment guarantee scheme and the food-for-work programme. Regarding that the Left leaders recalled having put up a detailed note to the Finance Ministry. The above-mentioned meeting had no visible sign of a breakthrough—the first with Sonia since the Left wrote to her informing of their decision to suspend their participation in the UPA-Left coordination panel over the Government's decision to disinvest BHEL. Sonia's emphasis on finding a 'way' to settle the matter as early as possible held out some hope of a resolution. They finally ended boycott when Sonia informed them that the Government has withdrawn the BHEL proposal.

The coalition government has been doing a 'magnificent job' especially for the *aam admi* in translating the basic and important goal of the NCMP. Keeping with the 'sensitivities' of the coalition partners the Prime Minister put on hold the disinvestments decision of some Government undertakings though the proposals were related to profit-making non-

Navratna PSUs as allowed under the NCMP. The Centre's decision came after DMK's Karunanidhi got in touch with UPA Chairperson who in turn consulted the Prime Minister.

The Congress, however, doesn't think it succumbed to DMK's blackmailing. It saw the retreat as a temporary step pending discussions. The party maintains that it believes in true coalition dharma but taking into account diverse views of the coalition partners.

Despite differences over many issues, particularly on economic and foreign, the Left parties still want that the UPA Government run for full five years. CPI (M)'s Jyoti Basu and CPI's Bardhan gave an indication to this effect. "The Left parties would continue to support the UPA Government despite the present political scenario," said CPI General Secretary Bardhan. His reaction came over the possibility to form a 'third front' at the Centre in near future. "It is true that we have differences on economic and foreign policies under the present circumstances but the Left parties do not want the communal forces to emerge as an alternative to the present Government," he said. Even DMK's Karunanidhi has said that there was no threat to the UPA Government. According to him there was a systematic campaign going on to create a rift between the DMK and the UPA, thereby to dislodge the Government and that didn't materialise. However, the Left parties felt that it was good for the Government to 'jettison' the second generation of economic reforms while strictly adhere to the NCMP. Although Left parties were against the selling off of profit making PSUs, they had no problem for partial disinvestments from five to ten per cent on a case-to-case basis in some selected cases.

MATURE DECISION

Sonia made a matured decision by choosing Manmohan Singh for the prime minister's post. There is no doubt that he is the right man for the right post. But her rivals believe that she is the real power behind the throne. Allegations are being levelled against her that she is behaving above the Prime Minister. It is for their dismay that nothing till date suggest she ever publicly displayed any sense of superior power and for that matter, the desire to belittle the Prime Minister's Office.

It is pertinent to mention here an episode that both Manmohan Singh and Sonia were to visit New York at the same time on different missions. On the one hand, the Prime Minister had to attend high-level plenary meeting of the United Nations General Assembly and a meeting with US President George W. Bush on September 14, 2005. On the other hand, former US President Bill Clinton who planned his first 'global initiative', an unprecedented gathering of world leaders in New York from September 15-17, invited Sonia. She also decided to attend the meeting. The gathering was all about to aid Clinton's efforts to find solutions to some of the world's most pressing challenges. As it became a protocol problem for the Indian mission there, the Foreign Ministry was trying to find a way out. Several proposals were put forward to decide upon. One such proposal was that Prime Minister cut short his visit. If the proposal was to be accepted, he would have to arrive at New York on September 13 and leave on 15, the day Sonia's activities were to begin in the city. Because her visit clashed with the Prime Minister's, Sonia decided to cancel her own visit, only to save the Indian mission from its embarrassment.

Sonia doesn't have delusion that she is great or powerful, as some leaders of the rival parties believe. She always shows the Prime Minister impeccable respect. It is seen that she queue ups to see him off whenever he goes on a foreign visit. On that occasion also she keeps austerity in mind. While many greet the Prime Minister with bouquet, she does so with just a rose stalk.

There is no truth in the Opposition allegation that Sonia has belittled the office of the prime minister by creating two power centres. She has vehemently denied that there were two centres representing her and Prime Minister. "Those who talk of two power centres, don't know what they are talking about; the Prime Minister and I are in regular communication, we share a strong relationship and I have full faith in him," she said clearing the misconception once for all. About the

Government's performance she said, "The Prime Minister has done a fine job; I have no complaints whatsoever."

About Sonia, the Prime Minister, however, says that she is his source of inspiration and not weakness. His reaction came when media persons asked him whether she was more powerful. He, however, stated that as UPA Chairperson she wielded a 'legitimate' influence in the Government.

Under Sonia's leadership the Congress party has consolidated its base within the UPA. It carries greater clout within the UPA while the BJP's presence within the NDA has shrunk. According to the survey conducted around the second year of the UPA Government, the party has been on its perfect role. The Centre for the Study of the Developing Societies (CSDS) conducted the Hindustan Times-CNN-IBN State of the Nation poll. The findings show that the UPA Government enjoys comfortable lead of 10 percentage points over the NDA—a big leap since the last parliamentary elections when both the alliances had nearly the same share of votes. In the past 20 months there had been a 5.8 per cent swing in favour of the UPA, while the NDA lost 3.6 per cent. According to the survey about 24 per cent voters still prefer Sonia should be the future prime minister.

About six months later the same agency conducted another survey namely The Hindu-CNN-IBN. According to it, had the Lok Sabha elections were held at the beginning of August the UPA would have won a comfortable majority on its own. The survey predicted that the coalition's tally could have crossed 300 seats as against the 222 the Congress and its allies got in the 2004 elections. It, however, showed that NDA would have got 120 seats only in comparison to 189 seats in 2004. The reason given was basically the slide in NDA's support base. The UPA owes its gain entirely to the Congress party. The party was projected to get 240 seats on its own, slightly less from a simple majority. The survey projected worst performance for the NDA with 82 seats, lowest in 17 years. Several factors were mentioned that favoured the Congress. The first was the better Sonia-Manmohan Singh popularity rating. The leadership crisis within the BJP has left no one in a position to fill the void created by Vajpayee. In the second, the Congress has benefited from the nation-wide shift of the regional parties. The finding also shows that the Congress is beginning to regain some of the social grounds it lost in the 1990s. About Sonia's own popularity, it has gone up by 4 points over the previous rating about six months ago and improved slightly that was in 2004, from 27.2 to 27.9. The popularity of Manmohan Singh has also gone up by about 3.4 points over six months. Vajpayee's popularity, however, has gone down drastically, from 38.3 in 2004 to 18.5 presently, as per the survey.

According to the NDTV-MODE poll, more than 80 per cent of the respondents consider Manmohan Singh a very popular leader. The poll indicates that the Government has its sway over the electorate; notwithstanding the reverses it suffered in some Assembly elections. If the elections were held before the scheduled time, the Congress and its allies would sweep the polls. The latest survey by India Today-AC-Nielson-ORG-MARG reveals that as many as 35 per cent of the respondents felt that Manmohan Singh's performance was good while 40 per cent of them rated him as average. A majority of 55 per cent of the respondents felt that the Government would last full term while in a poll conducted six months ago, only 36 per cent had expressed this opinion. As many as 39 per cent of the people in the survey were of the view that they would vote for Congress-led coalition, followed by 33.6 per cent of the BJP and its allies. According to the survey projections, the Congress-led coalition is likely to win 252 to 261 seats if the Lok Sabha elections are held now. This marks a gain of about 20 seats from the opinion poll conducted six months ago.

The *Sunday Times* poll showed that a large section of respondents think that their qualities of lives have improved under the present Government. Over 70 per cent respondents appreciate Sonia's role in running the Government. Another opinion poll conducted by the paper six months later, just before the completion of half scheduled term of the Government, found that the people still believe their quality of life remained the same.

Sonia has her own vision and is making honest effort to give effective governance to the country. She has clear perspective on economic policies, such as the role of the state in a market-oriented economy, WTO, globalisation, social security, disinvestments etc. Several outstanding policies like REGS, Bharat Nirman, SSA etc. have been taken up with her initiatives.

Sonia has candidly acknowledged the need for allies in different circumstances and at the Hyderabad plenary the party's political resolution formally accepted the inevitability of coalition in a bid to keep communal parties out of power. She considers it as a 'national imperative' to battle out those parties that are detrimental for maintaining communal harmony in the country.

Sonia has also exhorted the party activists to remain unshakable in their resolve to serve the nation. She pointed out that the UPA Government had given a new direction to welfare policies, economy and society and would undo the damage caused by the previous regime. She has declared full backing to Prime Minister Manmohan Singh, a signal to those nursing prime ministerial ambitions. "In Dr Manmohan Singh, India has a prime minister of great learning, vast administrative experience and impeccable reputation," this is what she said at an AICC session held in the Capital.

Although the Congress-led coalition Government at the Centre is a new experience for the party, the Congress President has been trying to honour the people's verdict by implementing the NCMP in letter and spirit. Top priority has been given to common people's issues, besides honouring the party's as well as UPA's manifestoes.

Sonia best understands that the Left has no choice but to support the UPA Government. As part of the coalition principle she consults the Left parties but never let them give the impression that they are calling the shots. She has to accommodate their wishes to some extent but in no way compromise the Government's basic integrity and purpose. She acknowledges the need for allies keeping in mind the inevitability of coalitions for the future.

Sonia believes that only her party can ensure peace and harmony in the country and blamed the previous government for social discord during its tenure. After the formation of the UPA Government she accused the BJP of trying to subvert mandate by not accepting its rejection.

Sonia seems to have devoted her life to the service of the country. She is a rare and selfless patriot and is giving her time and energy to party work and in smooth running of the Government. Despite her busy schedule she never forgets the deprived. It is her identification to work for the needy and underprivileged and the spirit of dedication that Congress chief shows towards the *aam admi* she has won the hearts of millions of her countrymen.

Sonia has kept in mind the wishes dear to her husband and accomplishing his unfinished task like empowering people at the lowest level with a modern approach and entrepreneurship and social justice with dignity, no matter what their religion or caste may be.

HUMANE NATURE

To love humanity and to work for their betterment is Sonia's ultimate aim. India is a country with over 30 per cent of its population well below the poverty line. Sonia has come across many people during her several visits to remote areas who are living a indigent life. She always bears compassion for them. As a leader of consequence she is always concerned for their uplift.

The humanitarian nature of the Congress President is well-known. To help the needy to the extent possible she has fixed some time (generally one hour but may be extended by few more minutes if required) for people who are stuck with problems and find no way out. They can meet her on Wednesdays and Fridays between 5-6 p.m. She also calls upon people to devote themselves for the betterment of the poor and the needy and believes that those who care and serve the society are successful in all means.

Sonia is great in her own way. Service to others is foremost in her mind. It is evident that when any natural calamity such as earthquake, tsunami, flood, drought or cyclone affects any part of the country or any incident happens in which heavy casualty occurs Sonia tries to be there as early as possible to express sympathy with the affected people and ensure that the sufferers get proper medical treatment or prompt relief supplies.

Once Rajasthan was hit by severe drought. The Congress party was then ruling there. She visited the state and after reviewing the situation took initiative to send truckloads of grains for the people and waganloads of grass for the cattle. On her advice the Chief Minister started many developmental works. Half a decade later the state was again hit by severe drought and this time it was ruled by a non-Congress party. As she has the desire to serve people she visited the state and reviewed the relief measures. On knowing about discriminatory relief distribution and low payment of minimum wages to relief workers in the Congress-dominated areas, she called upon partymen to start movement against the mis-governance in the state.

Sonia has earned great popularity as a social activist for serving people affected by calamities in other parts of the country. When quake hit Gujarat she was with the affected people and virtually threw her heart and soul in engaging party workers to the relief work. The whole nation appreciated her effort and took note of her great zeal, sincerity and humaneness with which she dispatched relief material. All she did with total devotion and selflessness.

Sonia takes pleasure in helping the *aam admi* and readily becomes facilitator for any difficulty they face. She always favours amicable solution to disputes in which the poor are the victims and tries to safeguard workers' interests. With this attitude in mind she mediated between the Hero Honda Management and the workers side to find an amicable solution. The tricky controversy resulted after the management sacked some of its workers. She played similar role when delegation of Sonepat's Gohana victims led by Union Minister Selja called on her. She assured that everything would be done to rehabilitate them and it was done within few months. The upper caste villagers burnt down 60 houses of Dalits. Local

Dalit leaders said that an area non-Congress politician was involved.

Sonia has special love for the tribals and ensures that the party stands by their side whenever they are in difficulty. She, accompanied with Home Minister Shivraj Patil, came calling to Kalinga Nagar and shared grief and extended heart-felt sympathy to the families whose members were brutally killed when protesting against government's displacement proposal. The two leaders quickly announced an ex-gratia payment of Rs. 5 lakh to each of the families. Earlier she placed wreaths where the tribals were cremated. About 13 tribals were killed in police firing while protesting against the setting up of 10-million tonne steel plant.

GREAT SACRIFICE

Sonia is in politics to give shape to what Rajiv dreamt about India. She has made a good beginning to reach that goal but not at the cost of denigration. To keep her image unblemished she threw a bombshell on March 23, 2006 by resigning from the Lok Sabha seat as well as from the NAC on the issue of holding 'office of profit' remaining an MP. By her resignations she has again proved that she is no power hungry. This step of her is no doubt a great sacrifice. The move has given the Congress party an upper hand over the belligerent Opposition, particularly the BJP, which criticised her bitterly.

Announcing her resignation Sonia said, "Some people have been trying to create an atmosphere as if Government and Parliament are being used only to favour me. It has immensely hurt me. I have said earlier too that I have not joined politics and public life for any personal gain. I have resolved to protect the secular values of the country and society. This is why, upholding the ideals of public life and politics, as well as my personal belief, I resign from Lok Sabha membership and as Chairperson of the NAC. I have full confidence that my brothers and sisters in Rae Bareli as well as the entire country will understand my feelings."

The UPA Government set up the NAC in 2004 as an interface between the people and the Government on the implementation of the NCMP. The Government pays for the NAC. The Opposition parties charged that Sonia as NAC Chairperson enjoyed rank and status of a Cabinet minister. The Congress party clarified that she never got salary or parks and held a purely advisory role. Besides Congress, some other parties believe that NAC is not an office of profit. According to them the MPs are required to perform various public responsibilities by holding such positions.

To express loyalty and solidarity with Sonia, several Congress leaders also resigned. They are Karan Singh—Chairman of Indian Council for Cultural Relations and Kapila Vatsyayan—Chairperson of Indira Gandhi National Centre for Arts (both Rajya Sabha MPs) and Gurudas Kamat—MP from Mumbai. Jairam Ramesh and Jyotiraditya Scindhia also expressed their desire to resign.

As soon as the news of Sonia's resignation spread, several Congress Ministers at the Centre, CWC members, AICC office bearers, Chief Ministers and ordinary workers thronged 10, Janpath shouting pro-Sonia and anti-BJP slogans. Congress spokesperson Jayanthi Natarajan said, "Sonia has taken the moral high ground, something that the BJP can never do, as they have no morals. Does any other leader have the moral authority to do what Mrs Gandhi did today." Senior Congress leaders also hailed her resignations. Party General Secretary Janardhan Dwivedi termed it as a renunciation. Party workers gathered to stage protest demonstration. The atmosphere was so surcharged with emotions that large number of NSUI activists, Youth Congress cadres and party workers holding aloft banners, party flags and pictures of Sonia were hailing her for the sacrifice. They were chanting *Khali karo yeh raste, Sonia Gandhi ke vaaste* (clear the path for Sonia Gandhi), *Sonia to ek aandhi hai, doosri Indira Gandhi hai* (Sonia is a storm, a second Indira Gandhi). The show took the shape of a jamboree, complete with burning of effigies and sloganeering. Slogans like *Soniaji tum sangharsh karo, hum tumhare saath hain* (Sonia continue your struggle, we are with you) rent the air. Reactions were also demonstrated in other parts of the country. In Lucknow, Youth Congress cadres burnt effigy of

Vajpayee. In Bhubaneshwar, the party workers vent their ire by burning Advani's effigy. The angry party workers burnt both the leaders' effigies in Chennai. Similar protests were also held in Patna, Bhopal, Ahmedabad and Shimla.

The 'office of profit' issue, which began with the disqualification of SP leader Jaya Bachchan from the Rajya Sabha, snowballed into a major controversy. The EC code doesn't clearly spell out what constitutes 'office of profit'. Political parties were demanding that the Parliament define 'office of profit'. Some wanted amendments to existing Parliament (Prevention of Disqualification) Act, 1959 followed by comprehensive legislation defining the matter.

Refusing to become prime minister after the General election, this is the second time that Sonia checkmated the Opposition. On taking this step, Prime Minister Manmohan Singh said, "Sonia Gandhi is the country's tallest leader and has a rare commitment to moral values which you don't find in plenty in our country." However, the BJP harped a different tune. Its President Rajnath Singh said, "Since Sonia Gandhi couldn't muster the courage to face Parliament or the EC, she sought to draw the curtains on misdeeds of the Government and divert public attention by resigning."

Many people considered Sonia's resignation as 'sacrifice' and not a compulsion. They believed that she had played a political masterstroke to checkmate her opponents. Many thought she had emerged politically wise and stronger. However, some described her move as uncalled for. BJP general secretary Arun Jaitley termed it as "desperate attempt to save her face after being caught red-handed trying to subvert the Constitution and Parliament".

Subsequently Sonia resigned from all the socio-cultural organisations she headed. By her rare example of sacrifice she proved herself something that the Opposition failed to understand. What her critics didn't realise is that Sonia is in politics not for power or position. The NAC position is a small thing for her in comparison to prime ministership, which she renounced earlier. It is her ardent desire to serve the people that she was holding the NAC post and in future will continue to hold positions like this. It is needless to say that through the NAC post she was performing advisory role for the Government with the sole aim of doing greater good for the people.

Since its inception the NAC had held over 20 meetings. It always took close look at various schemes launched by the Government and had widespread consultations with experts, NGOs and nodal ministries to draw mechanisms about how to keep flow of funds running so that the schemes could be run efficiently and in a result-oriented manner. It also took note of the analysis of the causes of gap between rich and poor states as well as problems faces by the less-developed states.

By her resignation Sonia has introduced a new trend of politics, which is rarely noticed in the present-day politicians. It is this trend that attracts some Congress leaders to emulate her with instinct of selflessness. By resigning she admitted that there might be something wrong and for which it was right time to take action. The Congress President, through her action, has put the choice to the people about what kind of politician they will like to have. Sonia's resignation has induced a new element of trustworthiness and values in politics. RSS ideologue and journalist M.G. Vaidhya said that her resignation has calmed down the Opposition parties, particularly the BJP. "By her resignation Sonia has shown her political skill and mature sense of politics," he said in his column of a Marathi daily *Tarun Bharat*.

RAE BARELI VISIT

After her resignation from the Lok Sabha seat as well as from the post of Chairperson of the NAC in the wake of the 'office of profit' controversy Sonia visited the Rae Bareli constituency to tell the people why she had resigned. In her address she said, "I am the Opposition's 'Enemy No. 1' target and every stone is being hurled at me." She told them that she had entered politics to serve the masses and that she faced lot of difficulties in her solemn endeavour. "I know that my path will be full of thorns but I can assure you that I am not going to lose and retract my steps," she said.

Recalling what compelled her to resign, Sonia said the Opposition parties had created an atmosphere that the Government was circumventing rules and regulations only to enable her to hold a position. "I consulted Rahul and Priyanka and we decided that I must resign to silence the critics. The people of Rae Bareli are members of the family and I want to assure that I will again contest from here," she said amid thunderous applause. Striking an emotional chord with the people she said straight to those who had sent her to the Lok Sabha, "I am sure you will do justice and give them a befitting reply." The crowd reciprocated. "*Hum nischit karenge ki jo bhi unke khilaf ladrenge, unke jamanat jabt ho jaye* (We will ensure that those whoever contest against her, lose their deposit)" was the general refrain.

Sonia said, without naming the BJP, "*Agar bijli bhi girti hai to yeh log kehte hain ki Sonia ki wajah se giri hai* (even if there is lightning, they say it is due to Sonia Gandhi)."

Sonia took a dig saying that after her resignation from the Lok Sabha, the Opposition parties had stopped speaking about 'morality' and were asking the Government to amend the law so that their party leaders could hold positions while continuing as parliamentarians or legislators.

Citing the names of members of Nehru-Gandhi family, she said that right from Pt Motilal Nehru to Rajiv Gandhi each one of them served the nation and sacrificed their lives for it. Despite their services, they had to bear the Opposition's onslaught regularly. She said the Congress was not merely a political party. It was a way of life, a movement for the people. She assured that she would continue to uphold the principles for which the members of the dynasty always stood. "I will continue to fight against injustice, against subjugation," she added.

Sonia maintained that as an area MP it was her duty to explain the reason behind her resignation. "First of all I discussed the issue with my children then I have come to you to explain the reason." She claimed that the NAC was formed aimed at implementing the NCMP of the UPA Government.

"*Jung jaari rahegi, caravan badhta rahega* (the fight will continue, the journey will progress)," Sonia said.

Slogans of "*Rae Bareli ka yeh tufan, badle saara Hindustan* (Rae Bareli's storm will change India)", *NDA walon hosh main aao, Sonia ji se na takrao* (NDA come to your senses, don't lock horns with Sonia)" and "*Tyag ki andhi Sonia Gandhi* (Sonia is the storm of sacrifice)", "*Soniaji ki pehchan, tyag, tapasya aur balidan* (Sonia's symbol renunciation, hard work and sacrifice)" rent the air.

Before entering Rae Bareli Sonia sought divine blessings. She visited Lord Hanuman temple at Churuah on the Lucknow-Rae Bareli border. After seeking blessings from the presiding deity of the temple, she also interacted with the people and accepted their greetings with folded hands. She also made impromptu stopovers at several spots along her route to interact with avid supporters, who chanted pro-Sonia slogans and showered her with petals. On the road thousands of people were surging ahead to get a glimpse of her when her motorcade passed through.

Sonia filing nomination papers for by-election to Rae Bareli Parliamentary constituency

In less than a month Sonia filed her nomination papers for the by-election of the constituency. Rahul and Priyanka were present on the occasion. Talking about the attachment of the Gandhis' with the people of Rae Bareli, she observed that the constituency was the 'Karmabhoomi' for the family and it was dedicated to the development of the area. Before filing the nominations she took blessings from the Lord Hanuman temple at Churuah.

Sonia appointed Rahul the election manager for the by-election. The high command gave him free hand to go his own way. Even the party advised the senior leaders not to go to Rae Bareli for campaigning as many had expressed their willingness to do so. The party believed that Rahul was capable enough of doing things on his own and needs no outside support.

It is pertinent to mention that Rahul is a tremendous crowd gatherer and very energetic. He has the quality to be an effective leader as he already had exhibited his confidence and maturity on several occasions. His presence in the constituency was giving sleepless nights to Sonia's rivals—be it BJP's Vinay Katiyar, SP's Raj Kumar Chowdhury or Apna Dal's Prabha Singh.

Sonia appointed her daughter Priyanka Vadra as election agent. While Rahul looked after campaigning, Priyanka handled administrative part of the electioneering. The high point was that she depended entirely on the family members and by any stretch it boosted her recognition as a mighty leader who will fight with a small force and even then cannot to be defeated so easily.

Sonia campaigned only for two days in the constituency. She declared war on her rival parties and castigated them for making undignified remarks. Her remark was for Mulayam who said that she had done nothing for her constituency. "I got a message urging me not to come. Yet, how can I keep away from my people when I visit all corners of the country," she said. With Rahul and Priyanka by her side she addressed meeting at Sareni, Sataon and Rae Bareli. She alleged that

Mulayam Singh government didn't use the Central fund thinking that its projects would give her party undue political advantage and told the people that his government refused to accept a Rs. 265 crore Central project for the Indira Gandhi Canal in Rae Bareli, which move would certainly create problems for the people. She asserted that better Centre-UP relations could help in the overall development of the state. Sonia reminded the people of the long-standing association with the Nehru Gandhi family saying Pt Nehru, Indira Gandhi and Rajiv Gandhi always strived for the development of India as well as Rae Bareli and said she needn't come to the constituency just for campaigning. Besides the Centre-UP relations, the issue of women's empowerment and their role in moulding future society also remained the focus of her address.

Lambasting the Opposition, Sonia said that she couldn't be cowed down by throwing canards against her. She sought the cooperation of the voters in her fight to serve the people better and work for the development of the country.

Next day Sonia addressed two meetings—one at Shankarpur and the other at Maharajganj assembly segments of her constituency. In the first meeting she pinned the future of national politics to the results of the by-election to the Lok Sabha seat. She declared that she was not in the town just for seeking support. The election was not an ordinary one but the one that would decide the direction of the future course of national politics. She, however, didn't elaborate it further.

Sonia is a campaigner for just and rightful causes and assured the people that she would continue her crusade against injustice and repression of the poor. She reminded the electorate that as long as they were with her, she was not afraid of anything.

Rahul was spearheading the campaign. Not caring the scorching summer heat, he visited remote villages sometimes by jeep, sometimes on foot and made crisp appeal to the voters for doing his mother a favour. He adapted himself with the locals so nicely that it was unimaginable for anyone what he did.

The election passed off peacefully. Only 43 per cent could cast their votes. The low turnout was due to high temperature of the month of May. There were altogether 16 candidates in the poll arena. It was felt that Sonia's winning margin will be very low but as was expected when the results were out she won it with record margin. All her rival candidates forfeited their security deposits.

Sonia polled 4,74,891 of the 5,90,026 votes, more than 80 per cent. It was the best performance so far in the rural constituency beating those of her husband Rajiv, mother-in-law Indira, father-in-law Feroze and her own winning margin of 2.48 lakh in 2004.

Acknowledging the victory Sonia thanked the Rae Bareli electorate and at the same time credited with equal measure to Rahul and the team who made it possible. As Rahul was election manager, he personally organised the campaign. He held roadside meetings and addressed village *chaupals* for almost 11 days. No doubt his hard work reflected in the result.

Sonia waving to her supporters at her residence after winning the Rae Bareli seat

There was jubilation among the supporters in both Rae Bareli and at Sonia's 10, Janpath residence. Delirious party workers were dancing to the tune of beating of drums amid bursting of firecrackers. Enthused supporters were also seen distributing sweets. In Rae Bareli, Rahul and Priyanka acknowledged the jubilant supporters by accepting *gulal* (coloured powder) and waving hands at the crowd from open jeep. They also thanked the electorate of the constituency for electing their mother for the second time.

On May 15 Sonia returned to Parliament as a new member, absolutely unblemished. There was sense of jubilation among the party MPs who thumped their desks as soon as she finished oath taking.

The Government, however, has made certain amendments in the Parliament (Prevention of Disqualification) Act. There are altogether 56 posts, which have been exempted from the purview of disqualification, including the NAC. The new law exempts offices of chairperson, president, vice-president or principal secretary or secretary of the Governing Body of any society registered under the Societies Registration Act, 1860, or any other law relating to the registration of societies.

About a month later Sonia again visited Rae Bareli to thank the people for electing her again as MP from the constituency with a record margin. Speaking at the *Abhar Samaroh* organised at the Firoz Gandhi College as part of the thanksgiving ceremony for booth-level workers she reminded them that a party could grow on the strength of its workers and not leaders. "Show the same spirit and enthusiasm as you did in re-electing me and take the message to the entire state as well as the country where elections are due," she urged the workers.

Sonia attacked the state government for obstructing development. During her two-day visit she came across the people's problems, mainly power supply. She assured that she would look into it. Stressing the need to generate more employment opportunities she also said that one large-scale industry would be set up in the area to deal with the unemployment problem.

The UPA Chairperson took particular interest to ameliorate the sufferings of the *aam admi* living in the rural areas. As CPP Chairperson, she also directed her MPs to remain concerned about the difficulties of the common people. She expressed her apprehension about the free-flow of funds to the Government's flagship programmes like Rural Employment Guarantee Scheme, Bharat Nirman, National Rural Health Mission etc. So she called for strengthening tax collection system, curtail unproductive expenditure, curb on wasteful utilisation of resources in order to raise fund for the programmes. The effect of these programmes will be felt at the grass-roots level.

Sonia best realises that the party cadres at district level can properly monitor the central schemes. For smooth functioning of the NREGS, she called in New Delhi 200 District Congress Committee heads where the scheme was being implemented and told them to closely monitor the implementation of the Act. It has come to the notice of the Centre that the Opposition-ruled states claim credit for the scheme.

Some states have supplanted the word 'National' with the name of the state on the job card issued under the scheme. Apparently concerned over the Opposition taking credit Sonia asked partymen to be aggressive in reaching out to the people to impress upon them that it was a Congress programme. The Prime Minister also addressed the gathering. "I appeal to you to go to the people and tell them that this right of employment has been given to them by Sonia and the Congress party," he said.

Sonia said at the day-long convention that the ambitious scheme was only in the Congress manifesto and later taken in the NCMP of the UPA. Both Manmohan Singh and Sonia emphasised that the Centre was giving 90 per cent of the funds for the 'revolutionary' scheme. "The legislation is historic. This is because nowhere in the world such an Act was there. It is for the first time that our Government has given legal right to employment to workers living in rural areas," the Prime Minister said.

Sonia said that the Congress party never discriminated states on political grounds. No wonder, a sizeable section of the beneficiaries of the rural employment programme were in Opposition-ruled states. "There should be no politics in the matter of development," she said and called upon party workers in these states to put the correct picture of the programme before the people and remain vigilant to see that it was properly implemented. "Any Government scheme can succeed only with the participation of the party," she told them.

The Congress President said that in the states where the party was not in power and the NREGS operation in place, it was the duty of the leaders to maintain a 'live contact' with the workers to keep themselves informed about its proper implementation. She informed that the report sent by the Government and the party about the progress of the scheme varied. This shouldn't be so. She called upon the ministers at the Centre and the states to keep touch with party workers and seek their cooperation sparing some time for them during their tours of different places. "The ministers could also visit the party offices during their tours. This will boost the morale of the party workers," she said.

Stressing the need for making an assessment of the NREGS, Sonia said if there was any shortcoming in the implementation, that had to be corrected. "We have to see that the scheme is benefiting the genuine unemployed and the wrong persons don't take advantage of it," she asked the partymen. The Congress President said the Panchayati Raj institutions and women of self-help groups could contribute their might in the proper implementation of the programme so that the scheme achieved its target.

About the coalition, Sonia said running a coalition Government was a great challenge and a task, which called for a great deal of patience and understanding. "There are challenges galore but under the able leadership of Manmohan Singh the Government is successfully facing the challenges," she said.

At the stock-taking session of the implementation of the Act many members demanded a monitoring committee and an amendment to the Law so that states couldn't replace the word 'National' in the programme. With Rs. 11,000 crore earmarked for NREGS—and Rs. 100 crore being pumped annually in every district, the battle for copyright to the programme is considered important. Almost 130 of the 200 districts fall in Opposition-ruled states. The grass-root workers of the Opposition-ruled states listed out the problems they face—corruption, favouritism, nepotism, contractor *raj*, non-payment of minimum wages and discrepancy in wage structures. Meanwhile, the Government is planning to extend the scheme to more districts of the country.

The NREGS would help in greening the barren rural roadsides. According to a fresh plan, poor workers to be assigned to plant trees on both sides of the 9,000 km long roads built under the Pradhan Mantri Gram Sadak Yojana. The workers to be paid for under the job guarantee scheme. The rural poor would also be able to take part in raising nurseries and planting trees.

Sonia has exhorted her MPs and party workers to closely monitor the working of the NREGS that touches the lives of the poor. The Congress chief feels the need for involving women and NOGs in social auditing of the developmental programmes. She wants that the people see this as a Congress initiative and prevent non-UPA parties from taking credit for the project. The concern attached to the exercise is borne out with the participation of CMs, CLP leaders, PCC chiefs, DCC presidents and AICC office bearers in the convention. With more than 500 participants, it almost turned into a mini AICC session. The crucial input came from grass-roots as the DCCs gave feedback on the implementation of the scheme.

In another address to Youth Congress activists Sonia asked them to reach out to the people at the grass-roots level and make them aware of party's policies. The occasion was gathering of Youth Congress district presidents named *Samvad* in the capital. She stressed upon the need to popularise policies of the Government, particularly the NREGS, RTI Act and SSA and said that youth were the future of the country, so they should come forward to help the needy and for the development of the country. They were also urged to strengthen the party base.

Congress President always nurtures genuine concern for the welfare, progress and happiness of the *aam admi*. Prices of essential commodities have been a matter of concern for the party President and took corrective steps timely. As the slogan goes *Congress ka haath, garibon ke saath,* Sonia wants to live to that image. She remains very much upset when the *aam admi* reel with burden of price rise and keeps herself fully updated about its impact. As the party is greatly concerned for the poor, she feels that the price hike of rice, flour, pulses, petrol, diesel etc. would surely put a heavy burden on them. Despite the Government spared kerosene and LPG prices from the rise, she urged it to keep the concern of the poor in mind and review hike to minimise the impact on them.

Getting into pro-active role on the issue, Sonia held discussion thrice with those who matter. She first called meeting of the CWC, the highest policy-making body of the party, to discuss the price rise and asked the Government to find a mechanism to manage the demand and supply of essential commodities. Besides the Prime Minister, the Finance Minister also attended the meeting. The Finance Minister detailed the meeting about the steps taken to check the price line. Next she called the AICC general secretaries in a meeting to receive inputs about the ground situation. From them she sought suggestions and means to bring the prices down so that the *aam admi* could be saved from the spiralling price rise. She also enquired about procurement of food grains, situation of the PDS and cases of hoarding and profiteering. She had yet another meeting with the party Chief Ministers to find means to check the price line and directed them to take strongest measures against hoarders, black marketeers and profiteers.

As an effective course to keep prices under control, the UPA Government took a slew of fiscal and monetary measures and efficient supply side management. It warned strict action against banks failing to give short-term farm loans at seven per cent credit within 48 hours of a complaint.

SOURCE OF INSPIRATION

Sonia has been showing enormous leadership ability in whatever position she is entrusted with. By far she is the most successful politician by any standard amongst the present breed. By her unique masterstroke and strategy she has brought about many turnarounds in the political sphere. As head of the UPA, which is a combination of 19 parties with common goal, she weilds immense clout to win over others and carry through complicated issues. With her initiative many Acts have seen the light of day, to name a few the NREGA and the RTI.

Under her the Congress party has not only become stronger but also remains united. What is noteworthy is that Sonia keeps the party leaders in a bind. The election results of various assemblies and local bodies turned out more or less on expected lines for the party. About running of the UPA Government despite pulls and pressures she is doing fine and as situation prevails it would last full term if the coalition and supporting partners are to be believed as they have expressed confidence many times in this regard. The most striking feature of the Government is that it has provided stability and maintained harmony in the country.

To keep the party unblemished and administration corruption-free, Sonia has directed senior leaders to stop culture of recommendation. To drive her point home she has asked the party general secretaries not to send recommendations to ministers on their pads. Not only this she has also ordered that access of selfish minded people to the party headquarters be controlled.

The Congress President has taken these steps because the party's top brass were receiving complaint of corruption resorted to by some leaders. The complaint was that the general secretaries put pressure on the ministers and in many cases they receive recommendation letters. It has also been noticed that several selfish persons easily enter the party headquarters and virtually create a market-like situation. Although officially no notice has been put up but the strong message has been conveyed. Except party leaders, workers and mediapersons, a time has been fixed for the outsiders.

On the other hand the top brass have also taken measures that the governments don't distance themselves from the *aam admi*. They very much create pleasant relations between the party and the governments. At the Hyderabad session the party President reminded those in the Cabinet that they shouldn't forget that they were in this position because of the ordinary workers. They have the responsibility towards the party workers and for that they need to keep in their mind the interests of the workers.

That there shouldn't be bitter understanding between those in the government and those in the party, both Prime Minister and Congress President remain wakeful in this regard. They don't want that frosty atmosphere prevail in the party. They believe that the sustainability of the UPA Government depends how peace is maintained in the party.

Arrangement for Complaint Cell has been made in the party headquarters with sittings twice a week. People from all over the country can register their grievances in the computer. Those list go directly to the party President. She goes through the list and those which she deems proper are sent to the concerned ministers for necessary steps. It has been ordered that no one should use the party office for personal benefit, except the established conduit.

Sonia always thinks for the well-being of the *aam admi*. With this in mind she has asked the ministers to visit their respective constituencies. They have been told to establish contact with the local people, hear their grievances and help them to what extent it is possible. If necessary they should visit the constituency once in a week.

On the occasion of completing two years in office Prime Minister Manmohan Singh along with Sonia released a report card detailing the achievements in various fields. Over a dozen senior ministers highlighted the initiatives taken by them in the thrust areas like agriculture, health, rural and infrastructure development besides steps taken in the flagship schemes like NREGS and Bharat Nirman programmes as envisaged in the NCMP. The Congress manifesto had promised the electorate 'transparency and accountability' as the USP of its governance.

The Congress President pledges to fulfil all the promises made under the NCMP.

In her speech Sonia said that the UPA was not just a collection of political parties. It was the idea that reflected the very nature of the society and polity. She said that challenges in the agriculture sector imposed an urgent and special responsibility on the Government. She admitted that there were different perspectives at times with other coalition allies. "These are inevitable but all are steadfast in the pursuit for ensuring a secular and pluralistic society," she said.

The credit for success of the UPA Government goes to a great extent to Sonia who remains instrumental in holding negotiations with the coalition partners, particularly the Left whenever differences persist. The Left parties always criticise Government in matters of economic and foreign policy and accuse it of deviating from the NCMP. That the Congress party is doing a good job, the Left parties have decided not to disturb the Manmohan Singh Government.

As Chairperson of the UPA, Sonia has tried to provide a responsive and clean Government. Her greatest success is the launching of the job guarantee scheme. She along with Manmohan Singh runs the responsive Government and people are generally satisfied with the performance of the regime. Several opinion polls conducted by the media houses show that the respondents think the Government will complete full term.

The Left parties have come out with their own critique of the UPA rule. They have abundance of bouquets and brickbats. The brickbats are on issues closer to their hearts like agriculture, food-prices, and energy policy. In so far the bouquets are concerned, these have come for steps that the Government took such as abolition of POTA, RIT Act, NREGA, new initiative on Kashmir and protection of the rights of the tribal people in their traditional lands. They want the Government to take some more pro-people measures, saying these are insufficient.

These parties' unfulfilled wish list includes women reservation bill. They also came down heavily on the Planning Commission saying it had become a hub for the initiation and pushing of policies that were contrary to the spirit of the NCMP. On the domestic scene it voiced unhappiness with the agrarian policy saying farmers' suicide continued at a disturbing rate and rural unemployment was increasing.

Sonia serves as a barometer for the Government and advises it whenever she finds any variance of the norms. She always remains alive to the difficulties of the farmers and that is why she has advised the Government to keep a watch on price and import of wheat. She has asked it to implement the recommendations of the Farmers Commission and also address the social security issues for unorganised sector workers.

Congress President is happy with the success of the UPA Government and even congratulated the Prime Minister on completing two years. Sonia is of the view that the Government's achievements be propagated and for this she has asked the Ministers and party leaders to remain better informed.

According to Sonia, the UPA Government has fulfilled its commitment by revolutionary measures like passage of NREG Act to confer the legal rights on the unemployed youth of the rural areas. Other important measures were taken to protect women from domestic violence. Appropriate legislations were passed to advance economic growth and foreign trade. These initiatives were launched in keeping with the promises made in the Congress manifesto and the NCMP. Now is the time for consolidation and ensure that these initiatives begin to show results.

Sonia has set high standards of value-based politics by resigning from the Lok Sabha on the issue of 'office of profit'. Her resignation is an indication that she can go to any extent to maintain and safeguard her image as a clean politician. After re-election from the Rae Bareli constituency her leadership got a boost and it is hoped that she would continue to serve the country with more dedication and perseverance to fulfil what Rajiv dreamt to see India in the 21st century. She has already declared that her commitment is to vigorously work for the welfare of every strata of society to build a strong nation.

The high point is that India's image in the comity of nations has received a major boost after the UPA came to power. The country has also achieved economic progress under its rule besides ensuring rule of law and providing transparency in the functioning of the Government.

Sonia's actions speak louder than words. She has provided a regime that proves to be a bliss for the *aam admi* and it is one of the reasons that her popularity has increased steadily. The days are not far when she will emerge more stronger and head a more strong government so as to lead the country at its tremendous height of growth.

You be a source of inspiration for partymen all the time and continue to serve the country for a long time—this is what I wish.

❑❑❑